UBLIC

DATE DUE			

ALSO BY HERBERT APTHEKER

American Negro Slave Revolts (1943)
Essays in the History of the American Negro (1945)
The Negro People in America:A Critique of Myrdal's 'American Dilemma' (1947)
To Be Free:Studies in Afro-American History (1948)
Laureates of Imperialism:Big Business Re-Writes American History (1954)
History and Reality (1955)
Toward Negro Freedom (1956)
The Truth about Hungary (1957)
The Colonial Era (1959)
The American Revolution (1960)
The World of C. Wright Mills (1960)
Dare We Be Free? The Meaning of the Attempt to Outlaw the Communist Party (1961)
American Foreign Policy and the Cold War (1962)
Soul of the Republic:The Negro Today (1964)
Mission to Hanoi (1966)
Nat Turner's Slave Rebellion (1966)
The Nature of Democracy, Freedom and Revolution (1967)
The Urgency of Marxist-Christian Dialogue (1970)
Afro-American History:The Modern Era (1971)
An Annotated Bibliography of the Published Writings of W.E.B.Du Bois (1973)

EDITED BY HERBERT APTHEKER

A Documentary History of the Negro People in the United States: From the Colonial Period to the Establishment of the NAACP (1951)
Disarmament and the American Economy (1960)
And Why Not Every Man? A History of the Struggle against Slavery (1961)
Marxism and Democracy (1964)
Marxism and Alienation (1965)
One Continual Cry:David Walker's 'Appeal to Colored Citizens' (1965)
Marxism and Christianity (1968)
Autobiography of W.E.B.Du Bois (1968)
The Correspondence of W.E.B.Du Bois (Vol.I,1879–1934) (1973) (Vol.II, 1934–1944) (1976) (Vol.III, 1944–1963) (forthcoming)
The Education of Black People, by W.E.B.Du Bois (1973)
A Documentary History of the Negro People in the United States: From the Emergence of the NAACP to the Beginning of the New Deal (1973)
A Documentary History of the Negro People in the United States: From the Beginning of the New Deal to the End of the Second World War (1974)
The Published Writings of W.E.B. Du Bois; 20 of 40 volumes published as of 1976.

A History of the American People

EARLY YEARS of the REPUBLIC

*From the End of the Revolution to the
First Administration of Washington (1783-1793)*

by Herbert Aptheker

International Publishers, New York

320.9733
Ap8e
103263
Dec. 1977

LIBRARY OF CONGRESS CATALOGING IN PUBLICATION DATA

Aptheker, Herbert, 1915–
    Early years of the Republic.

    (His A history of the American people)
    Bibliography: p.
    Includes index.
    1. United States—Politics and government—1783–
1789. 2. United States—Politics and government—
Constitutional period—1789–1809. I. Title. II. Series.
E303.A67   320'.9733'18   76-40213
ISBN 0-7178-0480-1
ISBN 0-7178-0471-2 pbk.

To Jennifer and all the years ahead

The author expresses deep appreciation for the kindness of Professor Sidney Kaplan who read the entire manuscript and made important corrections and suggestions. Remaining failures are mine alone—H.A.

CONTENTS

EARLY YEARS of the REPUBLIC

Chapter I

The Articles of Confederation:
Source and Nature

THE IMMEDIATE source of the Declaration of Independence creating the United States of America was a Resolution offered to the Continental Congress on June 7, 1776, by Richard Henry Lee, of Virginia, urging a three-fold, interrelated program: 1) independence; 2) foreign alliances; 3) confederation.

To achieve the first objective, it was necessary to realize the second; to achieve the second, some single, united governmental body obviously was to be preferred over thirteen separate ones. Further, to gain independence required effective war measures and these were impossible so long as a centralized body, with the needed means and authority, did not exist.

Such was the logic of Lee's historic Resolution. The achievement of the first and second portions of the Resolution were considered in an earlier volume; it remains to follow the course of development of the third. The pertinent section of the Resolution read as follows: "*That a plan of confederation be prepared and transmitted to the respective Colonies for their consideration and approbation.*"

Four days later, the Congress appointed a small committee, headed by the conservative John Dickinson, late of Philadelphia, then of Delaware, and including Samuel Adams of Massachusetts, Roger Sherman of Connecticut and John Rutledge of South Carolina, to prepare such a plan. In one month, on July 12, 1776, the Committee submitted to Congress the original draft of the "Articles of Confederation and Perpetual Union." This draft was debated for about five weeks, and then laid over by Congress until the following spring; it was taken up again in April, 1777 and debated from time to time thereafter until adopted in mid-November, 1777. Then it was sent to the State legislatures with a circular asking for prompt action, and apologizing for Congress' tardiness. This last was explained on the grounds:

> that to form a permanent union, accommodated to the opinions and wishes of the delegates of so many states, differing in habits, produce, commerce, and internal police, was found to be a work which nothing but time and reflection, conspiring with a disposition to conciliate, could mature and accomplish.

Six states—Massachusetts, Rhode Island, Connecticut, New York, Virginia and South Carolina—did act promptly, ratifying the Articles before the close of 1777. But others acted more slowly—Pennsylvania, North Carolina, Georgia and New Hampshire not ratifying until the summer of 1778; New Jersey in November of that year, Delaware early the next, and Maryland not until March, 1781.

Let us indicate first the contents of the Articles as finally adopted and ratified; then we shall revert to the substance of the debates in the Congress and in the State legislatures which accounts for the five-year interval between original proposal and final ratification.

There were thirteen articles in this first Constitution of the United States; together they came to about 7,000 words, considerably less than the Constitution drafted in 1787. Here, officially, to begin with, the new Republic was styled "The United States of America." The retention by each state making up the confederation of "its sovereignty, freedom and independence" was made explicit; the confederation itself was called "a firm league of friendship" entered into: "for their common defence, the security of their liberties, and their mutual and general welfare . . . ."

The citizens of one State were declared to have the rights of citizens of other States, with unfettered entrance and departure; extradition was provided for as was the honoring of the acts of judicial proceedings of each state by all the others.

Delegates to the Congress were to be selected annually by the States (and paid by them); no State was to have more than seven nor fewer than two delegates, but each State was to have one and only one vote. They were to enjoy absolute freedom of speech and debate within Congress, and were to be immune from arrest while in the performance of their official duties.

No titles of nobility were to be granted by the Congress; no officer of the United States was to accept any position or title from a foreign power; no State was to enter into diplomatic or commercial agreements with any foreign power, without the express permission of the Congress. Two or more States were not to enter into any treaty or confederation or alliance, between or among themselves, without the consent of the Congress. Duties or imposts violative of any treaty entered into by Congress were not to be laid by any State. ·

Neither naval vessels nor armies were to be maintained by any State, in time of peace, except as allowed by Congress; but every State was to maintain "a well-regulated and disciplined militia." No State was to engage in war without the consent of Congress. When land forces were raised by any State in the common defence, all officers from Colonel down were to be appointed by the State; general officers were to be appointed by the Congress.

All expenses for war and defence and for the general welfare were to be met by a common treasury, the funds for which were to come from the States, "in proportion to the value of all land within each State"—but the actual levying of taxes was to be done only by the States.

Congress alone was to have the power of war and peace; of entering into treaties and alliances; of establishing admiralty courts and courts for settling interstate disputes; to regulate weights and measures and the value of coins; to regulate Indian affairs, if not within the borders of a particular State; and to conduct the post-office service. During the recesses of Congress, a Committee appointed by it and consisting of a delegate from each State was to conduct the functions of the government.

The Confederation pledged the redemption of all general debts. On major questions—war or peace; treaties and alliances; coining money; apportioning taxes; appointing a Commander-in-Chief—the assent of nine out of the thirteen States was required; on other points only a majority was needed. A process of amendment was included as the final article of this Constitution, but it was an exceedingly difficult one:

> nor shall any alteration at any time hereafter be made in any of them [the Articles, that is]; unless such alteration be agreed to in a Congress of the United States, and be afterwards confirmed by the legislature of every State.

In summary, the Articles did provide for a general government; it did forbid the formation of any other confederations; it did have the exclusive power of war and peace; it alone could make treaties and alliances and conduct foreign affairs; it alone could coin money and set the standards of weights and measures; it alone could conduct postal affairs; it had large responsibilities in relation to the Indians; it was charged with paying the debt incurred in conducting the Revolution; and it alone could maintain an army and navy.

Under the Articles, however, the Congress dealt directly with the States, not with individuals and, generally speaking, had nothing whatsoever to do with the citizens of the United States as such (the only exception being that it forbade the appearance of a nobility). John Adams was wrong, as Jefferson did not fail to tell him, when he held the Congress to be only a "diplomatic assemblage"; but Adams was pointing to a significant reality, namely, that the Articles did set up a "league of friendship" of sovereign and independent States. Under the Articles, the Congress did depend upon the States for the *execution* of those measures it might lawfully adopt. Furthermore, in three major areas its powers were absent: Congress could not lay taxes; it could not regulate commerce; and there was no authority in the Congress so far as the western lands were concerned.

There already appeared, in the debates on the original Dickinson draft of the Articles, cleavages which reflected fundamental differences concerning theories of government; these differences, in turn, basically arose out of differences in economic and social backgrounds.

On the whole, the tendency of the commercial and industrial and financial bourgeoisie—the latter two, in particular, present in rudimentary form—was towards the nationalizing of the market and therefore towards nationalizing the polity. The petty bourgeoisie, especially the farmers who then constituted so large a portion of the white population, operated within a more localized economy and tended not only to reject the need for more expanded outlets but to be suspicious of those who sought them. The suspicions were enhanced because one of the grievances producing the Revolution was the British effort to centralize the government of the colonies at Whitehall. It was felt that efforts towards centralization of government—especially over extended areas—carried with them the danger, if not the purpose, of establishing political tyranny.

The classical literature on politics had emphasized that the larger the governing unit the less possibility there was of direct democratic reality; it had insisted, too, that even representative democratic institutions required relatively limited areas, else the truly representative and the effectively democratic features of such institutions became more and more illusory.

Along with this, went the well-nigh universal view of government as the reflection or the demonstration of man's bad nature. Since governments had hitherto always been restraining and oppressive, it was assumed that this was due not to the specific class domination associated with all hitherto existing governments, but rather to the generalized and immutable failing of "human nature" per se. Therefore, political power in particular was held in the greatest suspicion. Thus, Thomas Burke, a Left-wing Revolutionist from North Carolina and a member of the Continental Congress, wrote the Governor of his State in March, 1776:

> The more experience I acquire, the stronger is my conviction that unlimited power can not be safely trusted to any man or set of men on earth . . . power of all kinds has an irresistible propensity to increase a desire for itself. It gives the passion of ambition a velocity which increases in its progress, and this is a passion which

> grows in proportion as it is gratified. . . . These and many other
> considerations make me earnestly wish that the power of Congress
> was accurately defined and that there were adequate checks
> provided to prevent any excess. . . . I believe, Sir, the root of the
> evil is deep in human nature. Its growth may be kept down but it
> cannot be entirely extirpated. Power will sometime or other be
> abused unless men are well watched, and checked by something
> they cannot remove when they please.

Yet, the necessities of war, and the reality of a national
unity—the consciousness of which sharpened as the fighting
progressed—plus the needs of diplomacy and commerce, developed a growing centralization of authority in fact; the creation
and adoption of the Articles represent a signal demonstration of
this truth. Of immediate importance, too, in the move towards
centralization, was the growing inflation, especially after 1778,
and the mounting military difficulties and setbacks, culminating
in 1780 in the British successes in South Carolina and their
consequent drive towards the north.

The neat balance of forces among Left, Center and Right in
the Revolutionary coalition manifested itself in the actual process of writing, debating and adopting the Articles. The document as it came from the hands of its chief drafter tended
toward a greater centralization in government than the Left was
willing to concede; the debates produced a considerable modifi-
cation in the direction of reducing the power of the Congress.
Yet the final document, as we have seen, was one which did
establish a central confederation; this, in turn, provided the
groundwork for something new in political history—a divided
and multiple sovereignty.

Specific changes in the Dickinson draft, forced through
Congressional debate, all went towards reducing the authority
of the central government. Thus, for example, while the Dickinson draft reserved to each State "as much of its present Laws,
Rights, and Customs as it may think fit, and . . . the sole and
exclusive Regulation and Government of its internal police," the
final document asserted in much more sweeping terms: "Each
State retains its sovereignty, freedom, and independence." The
Dickinson draft had given Congress authority over the Western

lands, the final document rescinded this; the draft had given Congress unlimited power in Indian affairs, the final document excluded Congress from such affairs whenever they fell exclusively within a State's boundaries; the draft had omitted control over funds and the appointment of a Commander-in-Chief from those areas requiring the consent of a full nine out of thirteen States, the final document added that requirement.

Care was taken in the final document to see to it that votes in Congress were by State—with each State having one vote—and not by population or property valuation. This, too, strengthened the "diplomatic" character of the Confederation; it was further enhanced by having the salaries of the delegates paid by the States.

Avoiding population as a source of voting in Congress and as a basis for fixing tax assessments brought out rather extensive debates over the institution of chattel slavery, and already demonstrated the differences over this institution to be of fundamental consequence in American politics. It was in the course of these debates that John Adams rather brutally disclosed normally masked upper-class feelings about the essential inferiority of the "poor" and those who labor; Adams insisted that the exploitative and oppressive reality of wage labor was little removed from that associated with chattel slavery. He thought, indeed, with a careless disregard for important details that reflected his own distance from either position, that except in words, the laborer in the North was as much a slave in fact as was the chattel in the South.

It was, too, in connection with this debate that Benjamin Franklin, dedicated foe of slavery, propounded as pregnant a question as has ever been put in parliamentary discourse. Discussing the question of the taxation of various forms of property, a delegate from Maryland permitted himself to remark that he could see no significant difference in such forms; hence, he thought, whether the property were slaves or sheep was of no moment. Franklin wondered if the Marylander would yield him the floor for a question which, he thought, might shed some light on the difference between two such forms of property. The floor was yielded, and the Pennsylvanian wanted to know if the delegate from Maryland could inform him when an insurrection of sheep had occurred?

The greatest obstacle in the way of confederation was the question of the Western lands. So thorny was this that it had not been resolved in debate, and the power of disposing of these lands was not granted in the Articles. Hence ratification of these Articles had to wait until the land disposition question was resolved by State action; it is this that fundamentally explains the lapse of time—from 1777 to 1781—between Congressional approval of the Articles and their ratification by the requisite number of State legislatures.

Involved here were major and conflicting interests in fur-trading, inland water commerce, and, above all, land-speculating companies. Present, too, was keen jealousy among the States themselves, some holding extensive Western lands, some moderate portions, and some none at all. Such holdings or their absence, had obvious meanings for the long-time future of the States; they were of immediate moment, too, for land grants to war veterans had been very common.

Six States—Massachusetts, Connecticut, Virginia, the Carolinas, and Georgia—had enormous land claims, based on colonial "sea to sea" charters. New York maintained considerable land claims on the basis of rather ambiguous Iroquois Indian titles. The remaining six States had no legal claims to the Western lands; they maintained, therefore, that all previous claims were without validity, and that, as a result of the War, the States collectively possessed all the Western lands (beyond their own borders) extending to the Mississippi River—recognized by Great Britain in the Paris peace treaty of 1783, as the western extremity of the United States.

The reluctance of the "landless" States to ratify the Articles placed pressure upon the others—needing, as they did, a national authority—to yield up their claims to the common title of the United States. The refusal of Maryland, in particular, to ratify the Articles unless the lands were disposed of in the manner indicated, finally won the day. Led by New York—whose land titles were quite cloudy, anyway—much of the

Western land claims were yielded. Of greatest consequence was the act of Virginia in giving up her claims to almost all her Western lands. Immediately with this announcement, Maryland, on March 1, 1781, ratified the Articles and they then officially went into force. By 1790 all of the land-title States, except Georgia, had yielded to the Union; and Georgia did by 1802. As a result, the Federal government obtained title to 250,000 square miles of territory, and this prior to the Louisiana Purchase.

It is impossible to exaggerate the consequence of this boundlessly rich, largely unsettled land for the history of the United States. At the moment, emphasis is placed upon the unifying force which the common ownership of this empire represented. That the thirteen States, so vast in size, so varied in populations, so diverse in economics, and so remote one from the other, would remain united seemed hardly likely. This was true quite independent of the fact that a significant strand of British diplomacy for a generation after the Revolution was taken up with dissolving the Union; and that disuniting tendencies also found support in Spanish interest as well as in the desires of those who wished ill for the great experiment in republican politics.

Pertinent to the first consideration was the prediction of Dr. Josiah Tucker, the Dean of Gloucester, an Englishman who was, as it happened, quite friendly to the new nation. Wrote the Dean in 1781:[1]

> As to the future grandeur of *America,* and its being a rising Empire, under *one head,* whether Republican, or Monarchical, it is one of the idlest, and most visionary Notions, that ever was conceived even by Writers of Romance. For there is nothing in the Genius of the People, the situation of their Country, or the Nature of their different Climates, which tends to countenance such a Supposition. On the contrary, every prognostic that can be formed from a Contemplation of their mutual antipathies, and clashing Interests, their difference of Governments, Habitudes, and Manners—plainly indicates that the *Americans* will have no *Center of Union* among them, and no common interest to pursue, when the Power and Government of *England* are finally removed. Moreover, when the Intersections and Divisions of their Country by great Bays of the Sea, and by vast Rivers, Lakes, and Ridges of

Mountains—and above all, when those immense inland Regions beyond the Back Settlements, which are still unexplored, are taken into Account, they form the highest Probability that the *Americans* never can be united into one compact Empire, under any species of Government whatsoever.

Nothing did more to defeat the Dean's apparently logical forecast—to supply that "center of union" and that "common interest"—than the common federal ownership of the Western lands.

There developed, too, an increasingly vital sentiment of nationality which more and more embraced a larger aspect than the borders of one's own State. This, as shown in *The Colonial Era*,[2] appeared prior to the Revolution, and was of consequence in the roots of that Revolution. It grew enormously because of that Revolution, and the experience of the Confederation, and the common ownership and settlement of the great West further fed the sentiment.

It is true that, for example, Fisher Ames, the Massachusetts conservative, wrote in 1782: "Instead of feeling as a nation, a state is our country. We look with indifference, often with hatred, fear and aversion, to the other states." Yet, it is noteworthy, that Ames was regretting this feeling, partially, no doubt, for purely political reasons; present, too, however, was a national feeling outraged at the persistence of particularity.

J. Allen Smith, in his *The Spirit of American Government* (1907), was perceptive when he suggested that one of the reasons for the absence of a strong central government in the Articles was "the lack of development of a strong sense of all round nationality." This is an important explanation often overlooked in more recent writings, notably that of Merrill Jensen, ascribing this absence solely to consciously political motivation. Yet, again, it is necessary to call attention to the fact that the Articles represented *at that time* an *advance* in terms of centralized power. Thus, the historical problem is not one confined to explaining the relative absence of centralized power in the Articles as compared with the Constitution; it is also one of explaining the advance in centralization represented by the adoption of the Articles.

To forces already touched upon, this one of developing

national feeling is quite important. In addition to the negative kind of evidence supplied in Fisher Ames' comments, one has evidence in the writings of Jefferson—who was surely not a spokesman for increased federal power because of antidemocratic tendencies. Jefferson, while passing through Boston on his way to Paris, wrote to Madison, July 1, 1784, that he found "the conviction growing strongly that nothing could preserve the Confederacy unless the bond of union, through common council, should be strengthened." Jefferson announced himself in accord with this conviction and explained:

> The interests of the states ought to be made joint in every possible instance, in order to cultivate the idea of our being one nation, and to multiply the instances in which the people shall look upon Congress as their head.

The appearance of a more naive national—not to say nationalistic—feeling is reflected in the diary entry of the United States Minister to Great Britain, John Adams, dated March 19, 1785. A foreign ambassador asked if Adams had been in England frequently; Adams replied that he had not, 1783 being the only other time. The friend pursued the thought by inquiring whether or not Adams had many relatives living in England? None at all, replied the American diplomat, and for a century and a half, he added, all the relatives of which he had taken any note lived in America. Adams continued:

> So that you see I have not one drop of blood in my veins but what is American. "Ay, we have seen," said he, "proof enough of that." This flattered me, no doubt, and I was vain enough to be pleased with it.

A consequential part of this developing nationalism, was the sense of a special mission for America. This, as noted in an earlier volume, played a prominent part in American and European sentiment during the course of the Revolution itself.[3] It is prominent in the same "cold" New Englander who was pleased with this flattery, one not ordinarily associated with the "visionary" Left in American life. But here is John Adams writing to Count Sarsfield in London, January 21, 1785, to say that were he less lazy he would devote ten years of his life investigating the various devices used throughout history to establish and maintain systems of human gradation and subjugation. He would like

> to see how far the division of mankind into patricians and plebeians, nobles and simples, is necessary and inevitable, and how far it is not. Nature has not made this discrimination [continues the Yankee to the Count!]. Art has done it. Art may then prevent it. Would it do good or evil to prevent it? I believe good, think what you will of it.

Adams went on to tell the Count he wanted "to see . . . no distinctions in society"; furthermore:

> I'll tell you what. I believe this many-headed beast,[4] the people, will some time or other, have wit enough to throw their riders; and if they should, they will put an end to an abundance of tricks with which they are now curbed and bitted, whipped and spurred.

One might note that Adams, in this letter, did not exclude the American people from those yet "curbed and bitted," though he was writing some years after the Revolution. Yet, it is certain that he did see in the United States a nation arising in which "the beast, the people" were coming closer to throwing their riders than ever before. He returned to the same question a year later—February 3, 1786—writing to the same Count, in these words:

> It has ever been my hobby-horse to see rising in America an empire of liberty, and a prospect of two or three hundred millions of freemen, without one noble or one king among them. You say it is impossible. If I should agree with you in this, I would still say, let us try the experiment, and preserve our equality as long as we can. A better system of education for the common people might preserve them long from such artificial inequalities as are prejudicial to society, by confounding the natural distinction of right and wrong, virtue and vice.

Further reflecting this sense of "special mission" is the fact that the United States was the center of experiments in Utopian Socialism; the earliest of these was led by Ann Lee (1736–1784), originally a working woman from Manchester, England, whose four children died in infancy. She migrated to the New World in 1774, worked as a domestic, affirmed a message from God, urged celibacy and the renunciation of private property. In and around the present Watervliet, New York, she attracted followers who called themselves the "first witnesses of the Gospel of Christ's Second Appearing" and insisted that Ann Lee *was* the second coming, thus projecting the idea of a Father and Mother God. From Ann Lee's work came the Shakers whose first communal society was established in Mount Lebanon, N.Y., in 1787; by 1794 there were eleven such communities in New York and New England and by the Civil War the Shakers had 6,000 members in nineteen different communities. They gradually lost their religious nature and were virtually extinct by the end of the nineteenth century. These utopian experiments—and especially that of the Shakers—had considerable influence upon the thinking of Marx and Engels, the latter in particular declaring in 1845 that the very existence of the communal Shaker colonies showed that societies could exist without the private ownership of the means of production.

Chapter II

From the Articles of
Confederation to the Constitution

A CENTRAL PROBLEM in the literature on the Confederation period revolves around its overall estimate and evaluation. The differences range from those who see the period as chaotic if not catastrophic to those who see it as a time of readjustment and healthy growth. These differences lead in turn to others, so that some view the Articles of Confederation as embodying in governmental form the essence of the Declaration of Independence, and see in the Constitution a triumph of reaction, if not of outright counterrevolution; others see the Articles as brewer or abettor of the (alleged) chaos and therefore as endangering the Revolution itself, whose continuity would be guaranteed by the Constitution. Considerable heat is generated in the course of this debate, no doubt because the issues involved are quite momentous; certainly, harsh charges of outright political bias and factional motivations are hurled about and these have not induced that calm supposedly indispensable to scholarly pursuits.

Some examples may be offered to illustrate and illuminate the nature of these differences. In secondary works, it is generally held that the first systematic elaboration of the view that the period of the Confederation was an era of unmitigated failure occurs in John Fiske's, *The Critical Period of American History,*

1783–1789, issued in 1888. But this is clearly an error for the
bulk of the first volume of John B. McMaster's *History of The
People of the United States* is taken up with what the author calls
"The Weakness of the Confederation" and "The Low State of
Trade and Commerce." McMaster's volume was published in
1883 and the 250 pages he devoted to the topics indicated
formed a basic source for the Fiske book.

The theme of these works is sufficiently indicated by the titles
already quoted, with the addition that Fiske called his fourth
chapter, "Drifting toward Anarchy."

The sharpness of the modern differences of opinion about
this era may be indicated by contrasting the remarks of two
professors. William F. Zornow, for example, stated:

> The day of Fiske's *Critical Period* has run its course. Recent
> writers are re-evaluating the Articles of Confederation in terms of
> their significant achievements rather than their failures.

Broadus Mitchell, on the other hand, wrote:

> In judging of the Confederation, extenuation is more suitable
> than defense. Marshal counterclaim as ingeniously as you will,
> John Fiske was right. The performance from Yorktown to the
> Constitution was abominable, and alert men of the time knew it.
> Obstacles to internal and external trade paralyzed the first step
> toward improvement. Competitive tariffs impoverished all and
> exacerbated political quarrels.

Most prominent of those recently associated with the Fiske
view are Richard B. Morris and Louis M. Hacker; outstanding
pioneer in challenging that view has been and remains Merrill
Jensen. Mr. Hacker insisted "that not only was the Confederation inadequate but that the Revolution was being perverted; the
Constitution saved both the American nation and the Revolution itself." Furthermore, he added, with some bitterness:

> It has become increasingly the fashion among recent historians
> to seek to rehabilitate the reputation of the American governments
> of 1775–1789 . . . This defense of the Congress and the Confeder-
> ation has really a political motivation; its purpose has been to
> minimize the emergency that led to the summoning of the Consti-
> tutional Convention and therefore to attack the Founding Fathers
> as enemies of the Revolution . . .

Richard B. Morris also tended to question the motives if not the methodology of those who differ with the Fiske view. He found that "some recent historians have implied that all this talk of crisis (during the Confederation) was part of a Federalist plot to pressure the public into granting strong powers to the Federal government." But, Morris was sure that "the dissenting historians have never successfully refuted the mountain of facts" which substantiates the "critical-period" concept. Morris added another thought concerning this question. He believed that the division of supporters and opponents of increased centralization of power into "radicals" and "conservatives" was quite false; the division should be between "particularists" and "nationalists," and if revolutionists were anywhere, they were among those who sought enhanced central power, for these were the ones seeking change and transformation.

The latter argument is somewhat disingenuous, for the defining quality of radicalism is not the seeking of change alone; necessary to the definition is the quality of the change sought— else there would be no distinction between a revolutionist and a counterrevolutionist. And the problem of attitude toward democracy—so central to any concept of radicalism—remains crucial in evaluating the meaning of increased centralization of governmental power, so far as the Americans of the eighteenth century were concerned. On this particular point, Jensen's insistence that, viewed from that epoch, centralization was considered antidemocratic is true; all contemporary evidence substantiates this and none contradicts it. This does not mean, as Jensen tends to convey, that only the Right favored enhanced powers for the central government, but it does mean that contemporaries viewed such enhancement as at least posing a threat to effective popular sovereignty.

Let us trace at this point the developing movement looking toward the enhancement of the power of the central government. This movement was not confined to those of any particular outlook or class position; indeed, the feeling for *some degree* of enhancement of the power of the central government seems to have been well-nigh unanimous. It is, however, a fact that the further Right one moves in politics, the more intense the desire for greatly enhanced powers for the central government. Even this, however, has an exception: the far Right in American life, which opposed or seriously doubted the viability in any case of republican government, desired not a stronger central government but rather the disruption of the United States and its replacement with a series of confederations, more or less subordinate to the influence of Great Britain. This threat was a serious one during the closing years of the eighteenth century, and is to be borne in mind in estimating the general meaning of strengthening the government of the United States at that time.

The threat of true counterrevolution, seeking monarchical restoration, was real, as the neglected work of Louise B. Dunbar demonstrated, and figures as influential as von Steuben and Nathaniel Gorham were seriously involved in such undertakings. Additionally, one finds Gouverneur Morris writing to General Nathaniel Greene in December, 1782:

> I have no hope that our union can subsist except in the form of an absolute monarchy and this does not seem to consist with the taste and temper of the people. The necessary consequence, if I am right, is that a separation must take place and consequently wars.

This is the same period, as was shown in another volume, of top-level efforts to inveigle Washington into defying Congress and accepting the position of a military dictator. Somewhat later, the mutterings of certain prominent New Englanders, like Theodore Sedgwick, in favor of the creation of two or three confederacies, instead of a united republic, became notorious. James Monroe, Benjamin Rush, and David Humphreys recorded their fears, from 1785 on, of the imminent collapse of the confederacy. Typical was the letter written from Philadelphia in October, 1786 by Rush to the English libertarian, Richard Price:

> Some of our enlightened men who begin to despair of a more complete union of the States in Congress have secretly proposed an Eastern, Middle and Southern Confederacy, to be united by an alliance offensive and defensive. These Confederacies, they say, will be united by nature, by interest, and by manners, and consequently they will be safe, agreeable and durable.

Involved in these schemes was the hand of Great Britain. Benjamin Franklin, with his unsurpassed sources of information on matters of diplomacy, particularly emphasized this fact following the signing of the Treaty of Paris. In December, 1783, writing to the President of Congress, he pleaded that it be remembered that though a treaty had been signed, the English Court was not reconciled "to its loss of us, but flatters itself with hopes that some change in the affairs of Europe or some disunion among ourselves may afford them an opportunity of recovering their dominion." Writing as late as May 12, 1784, Franklin insisted: "Britain has not yet well digested the loss of its dominion over us, and has still at time some flattering hopes of recovering it. Accidents," continued Franklin, "may increase those hopes, and encourage dangerous attempts."

The question of preserving the integrity of the new Republic was one of vital concern to adherents of democracy not only from the rather negative viewpoint of thwarting the conspiratorial and counterrevolutionary efforts of indigenous and foreign reactionaries; it was posed also from the positive point of view of safeguarding the experiment which would test the possibilities that, as we have seen, John Adams was projecting to his friend, the Count. Present, too, was the idea of the existence of the United States as vindicating the Age of Reason itself; William Blake, in his poem *America*, saw the Revolution as a mortal blow not only against the tyranny of kings, but against subjugation of all kinds, for he thought it heralded men's making real their "will for their own freedom." Richard Price, too, saw the Revolution in terms of its world meaning, and held the task of preserving the wholeness of the Confederation to be sacred; on its success depended, he thought, the worldwide triumph of the application of reason to government. In the success of its federating effort, also, Price saw the projection of a universal federation of states, which would herald the achievement of man's noblest aspiration—"*universal* peace."

If to considerations such as these, one adds the developing sense of nationalism—to which reference already has been made—then it is clear why, beginning about 1780, figures as distinct in their outlooks as Paine, Hamilton, Washington and Jefferson were urging more and more insistently the need for a strengthened central government.

Furthermore, there were practical questions of administration, diplomacy, trade, and internal growth—especially the settlement of the West—which made people of all shades of opinion, so long as they were part of the Revolutionary coalition, see the need for enhancing the powers of the United States.

Under the Articles it is a fact that to sustain the barest forms of national sovereignty became increasingly difficult. Basic was the absence of funds, without which very little, least of all a government, can function adequately. Thus, while $4,000,000 were due the Confederation from the States on July 1, 1781, only $50,000 came in; while $6,000,000 were due from the States on September 1, 1781, only $125,000 actually came in. Indeed, the Congress had difficulty paying rent for its offices; it did not have the ready cash to pay the messenger who brought it word of Cornwallis's surrender; it could not get together a quorum of members to ratify the Treaty of Peace within the time stipulated in the negotiations—hence the American ratification reached Paris one month past the deadline, although the British, for very good reasons, chose to overlook the delay and accept the ratification.

Two states, Georgia and Delaware, failed to send any delegates to Congress after the war ended; and while in the six years from the Treaty of Paris to the organization of the new government under the present Constitution, the States were entitled to a total of ninety-one delegates, there were rarely as many as twenty-five attending Congress. Lacking a quorum, the Congress was forced to adjourn time after time; there were periods when such enforced adjournments lasted for two weeks. A total of twenty delegates from seven states witnessed the resignation of Washington from his supreme command, while only twenty-three members, from eleven states, were finally mustered together to sign the Treaty of Paris.

It is this weakness that moved Jefferson to write to Governor Benjamin Harrison of Virginia, January 16, 1784, on the urgent need for action on a federal level and the extreme difficulty of accomplishing anything within the existent governmental framework. Jefferson mentioned specifically the need to push effectively for treaties of alliance and commerce; for the establishment of arsenals throughout the country, of posts and forts along the frontiers; for the handling of Indian affairs through purchase and treaty; for the disposition of the Western lands, and for the efficient conducting of everyday administrative needs.

Already cited has been Jefferson's letter to Madison, written in July, 1784, where he reported, with manifest approval, the growing consensus on the need for a strengthened government. The Left abroad also expressed fear lest the extreme weakness of the United States government result in discrediting the essential accomplishment of the Revolution—the establishment of a republic based on popular sovereignty. A prime example of this is the work of Richard Price, particularly his *Observations on the Importance of the American Revolution,* published in London in 1784. One of Price's main points was the need to assure the stability of that Revolution, if it was to be "the means of making it a benefit to the world"; he urged, therefore, the strengthening of the central government. As Carl B. Cone has shown, Price's work was read with care very widely in the United States, and brought warm praise from Jay, John Adams, Washington, Franklin and Jefferson, all of them agreeing on its central proposal. Jefferson, for instance, writing to Price on February 1, 1785, stated that Americans were becoming aware of the "want of power in the federal head"; he added that the need for enhancing that power was generally recognized.

Jefferson, in this letter, pointed to the weakness in United States commercial relations as a prime consideration behind the growing desire for strengthening federal power. At almost the same moment, the Duke of Dorset was writing (March 26, 1785) to the United States commissioners in London who were seeking a treaty of commerce with Great Britain:

> I have been instructed to learn from you, gentlemen, what is the real nature of the powers with which you are invested, whether you are merely commissioned by Congress, or whether you have received separate powers from the respective states. . . . The apparent determination of the respective states to regulate their own separate interests renders it absolutely necessary, towards forming a permanent system of commerce, that my court should be

informed how far the commissioners can be duly authorized to enter into any engagements with Great Britain, which it may not be in the power of any one of the states to render totally useless and inefficient.

In the drive towards a more highly centralized and stronger federal government, certain local and particular motives played a considerable role. This was true, for example, in Georgia notwithstanding the fact that its own State government was notably of the radical variety. This apparent paradox is resolved when it is understood that Georgia felt acutely the need for a strong power supplementing that of the local forces for Georgia bordered on Florida, then held by a Spain highly suspicious of the new Republic; also Indians within Georgia (and in Florida) presented a serious police and military problem to the sparsely settled State—considerations heightened by the fact that so large a proportion of the settlers were slaves.

In New Jersey, as another instance, there was also near-unanimity behind the movement for a stronger central government. A careful student of this period in the history of the State, Richard P. McCormick, reports: "Conspicuously absent from sectional dispute was the subject of the strengthening of the union, on which all groups were in agreement." Important here was the very high tax rate in the State, which it was felt a continental impost might relieve; situated as New Jersey was between the two great commercial centers of New York and Pennsylvania, such federal control of commerce could only be beneficial.

Finally, there is no question that another source of support behind the movement to enhance the power of the central government came from the well-to-do as an expression of their desire to safeguard private property, and the sanctity of contract; of their fear of popular sovereignty; and of their elitism and contempt for anything smacking of egalitarianism. Clearly, the richer merchants, speculators, landowners, and planters saw in a carefully contrived and greatly strengthened central government a bulwark for their privileged positions; a guarantee for their investments; a support for their planned speculations; and a means for repelling the dangerous political and economic experiments in popular control that were proceeding in half a dozen States and threatening in the remainder.

Albert J. Beveridge, in his *Life of Marshall*, put this development quite clearly. He remarked that a section of those who had led in the Revolution, "had come to think," after the fighting:

> that, at the very best, the crude ore of popular judgment could be made to enrich sound counsels only when passed through many screens that would rid it of the crudities of passion, whimsicality, interest, ignorance, and dishonesty, which, they believed, inhered in it. Such men esteemed less and less a people's government and valued more and more a good government. And the idea grew that this meant a government the principal purpose of which was to enforce order, facilitate business, and safeguard property.

That Right, antidemocratic pressure was present in the movement to strengthen the central government is undeniable, but this does not mean that that movement is to be characterized in those terms alone—which tends to be the position of Merrill Jensen and those who have adhered to his viewpoint. What is clear is that there were varying motives and different classes behind that movement; that therefore there were differences as to how far and in what form the union should be strengthened. It does mean, also, that there developed acute suspicion, within the Left, of the trend towards centralization of government, with some feeling that since it was almost impossible to separate the real control of the Right from that trend it would be better to stand opposed to it in any form or shape. The reality of this Right-wing, antidemocratic ingredient as a prominent feature of the drive towards centralization is obscured by Richard B. Morris and others who have joined him in a very sharp assault upon the Jensen position. But such sharp and indiscriminate attacks do not coincide with the historical reality anymore than does the assessment of the movement toward increased centralization as nothing but a Right-wing, counterrevolutionary plot.

Eighteenth century property owners, having led in a successful national revolution, were seeking the nationalization of their market, the eviction therefrom of the British and the consolidation of their own supremacy, preliminary to rapid forward strides on their part. At the same time, though of the eighteenth

century and so still a progressive and even revolutionary force
vis-a-vis feudal and imperial restrictions, there is present the
fundamentally antipopular, antidemocratic bias of private possessors of the means of production, of dominators of a system of
exploitation (whether based on chattel or wage labor, or, in this
case, a mixture of the two). Meanwhile, the majority of the
population, which was not among the rich, also cherished the
results of the Revolution, also had profound national feeling,
and also wished to assure the stability and the continuation of
their blood-bought Republic. Among them, however, was the
strong desire to limit the extent of centralization, to prevent the
capture of the strengthened central government by the Right, to
guarantee a strong democratic content to that enhanced central
government as they could, and to maintain also a considerable
degree of power in their local governments, especially where
democratic forces had managed to gain control of such local
governments.

A word of caution is in place at this point. While it is generally
true that opposition to highly concentrated power in a central
government was associated with a more democratic outlook, it is
not true that the particularists and localists were pro-democratic
in all cases. On the contrary, some of the objections raised
against the Constitution by certain localists were of a quite
antipopular nature; and in the Confederation period itself,
there were antidemocratic tendencies among some of the localists.

In an immediate sense, decisive to the working out of this
pattern were the contemporary economic and political developments; it was these which most directly affected the contemporaries, whose activities constitute the history we seek to describe
and analyze.

Concerning the economic realities of the Confederation period there were differences among those contemporaries; these
differences have persisted and been accentuated by later historians. The Fiske school, including its modern proponents, tend to
report catastrophic conditions which they ascribe to the inadequacies of the Articles; the Jensen school tends to see a period of

postwar readjustment and recovery, which it takes as proof of the adequacy of the Articles.

Once again, the truth, it is believed, lies with neither. The truth seems to be that there existed considerable economic difficulty from about 1781 until the end of 1786, but that this was by no means of a catastrophic quality; that there were certain forms of economic activity and certain geographic areas very much better off than others; that there had to be a period of postwar readjustment regardless of the nature of the central government; that there was a general recovery to prewar levels, and even better, by the end of 1787; and that, in general, the form of government in this period of capitalist and plantation enterprise was far from decisive (though not without some influence) in accounting for economic developments.

Political motivations colored the observations and the reports of contemporaries; those in Europe, and especially England, who lamented the success of the Revolution and hoped for the early demise of the new Republic, tended to see in the New World nothing but anarchy and misery. Others, devotedly partisan to the new effort, tended to report nothing but prosperity, order and contentment. Similarly, later commentators and historians have reflected their political orientation in their descriptions and analyses, with those favoring the Federalists following the Fiske view; those favoring the opposite side, inclining towards the contrary interpretation.

Jefferson wrote to Monroe from Paris, August 28, 1785: "The English papers are so incessantly repeating their lies about the tumult, the anarchy, the bankruptcies, and distress of America, that these ideas prevail very generally in Europe." He had written in a similar vein to other correspondents, one of whom, Charles Thomson, the secretary of Congress, replied to him from New York, April 6, 1786, in this manner:

> Notwithstanding the paragraphs with which the European papers are stuffed, and the pictures they have drawn of the distress of America I will venture to assert, that there is not upon the face of the earth a body of people more happy or rising into consequence with more rapid stride, than the Inhabitants of the United States of

America. Population is increasing, new settlements forming and
new manufactures establishing with a rapidity beyond conception.
And what is more, the people are well fed, well clad and well
housed.

Yet I will not say that all are contented. The merchants are
complaining that trade is dull, the farmer that wheat and other
produce are falling, the landlords that rent is lowering, the
speculists and extravagant that they are compelled to pay their
debts and the idle and vain that they cannot live at others' cost and
gratify their pride with articles of luxury.

James Madison, on the other hand, writing from Virginia
where the decline in prices of farm produce had had a particularly distressing effect, tended to emphasize dire economic
troubles. Thus, he reported to Jefferson one month after
Thomson's letter: "The internal situation of this State is growing
worse and worse. Our specie has vanished. The people are again
plunged into debt to the Merchants, and those circumstances
added to the fall of Tobacco in Europe and a probable combination among its chief purchasers here have produced" this
desperate state of affairs.

Finally, typical of the letters to Jefferson that fell somewhere
between the view of Thomson and that of Madison, was one
from David Humphreys, a member of the Connecticut assembly, written from Hartford in June, 1786:

Many people appear to be uneasy and to prognosticate revolu-
tions they hardly know how or why. A scarcity of money is
universally complained of. But to judge by the face of the country;
by the appearance of ease and plenty which are to be seen every
where, one would believe a great portion of the poverty and evils
complained of, must be imaginary.

These differences among contemporaries do not appear only
in their private correspondence; they appear, too, in writings
meant for public consumption. Two examples of this may be
offered. Benjamin Franklin contributed an essay entitled,
"Comfort for America, or Remarks on Her Real Situation,
Interests and Policy" to the leading United States magazine of
the time, the *American Museum* (Phila.); it was printed in the
January, 1787 issue. Wrote Franklin:

> I see in the newspapers of different states, complaints of hard times, deadness of trade, scarcity of money, etc., etc . . . let us take a cool view of the general state of our affairs, and perhaps the prospect will appear less gloomy than has been imagined . . . All who are acquainted with the old world must agree that in no part of it are the laboring poor so generally well fed, well clothed, well lodged, and well paid as in America.

Continuing the comparison of conditions for those who were not rich in Europe and in the United States, Franklin concluded that there was "abundant reason to bless divine providence for the evident and great difference in our favor, and be convinced that no nation known to us, enjoys a greater share of human felicity."[1]

John Jay, however, writing as late as 1788, in *An Address to the People of New York*, emphasized a general stagnation of trade, a very depressed condition of the fur-trading business in particular, and the existence of all sorts of restrictions placed by foreign powers against American commerce. His conclusion—written explicitly as one who urged the need for a very much strengthened federal government—was altogether gloomy:

> Our debts remain undiminished, and the interest on them accumulating—our credit abroad is nearly extinguished, and at home unrestored—they who had money have sent it beyond the reach of our laws, and scarcely any man can borrow of his neighbor. Nay, does not experience also tell us, that it is as difficult to pay as to borrow? That even our houses and lands cannot command money—that law suits and usurious contracts abound—that our farms sell on executions for less than half their value, and that distress in various forms, and in various ways, is approaching fast to the doors of our best citizens?

The standard of living among the 65 percent of the United States population that were neither slaves nor indentured servants nor Indians was superior to that of the majority of Europeans. This fact certainly was a legitimate refutation of the demagogic laments anent allegedly intolerable conditions existing here that came from adherents of monarchy, feudalism and aristocratic privileges. But there are two respects in which they did not meet the question: 1) what was the reality of economic conditions here during the Confederation, not compared with Europe, but in terms of the experiences of Americans themselves; and 2) how relevant were the provisions of the Articles so far as these conditions were concerned?

As to the first, by and large there was a considerable post-war recession, starting about 1781, reaching its bottom sometime in 1786, beginning an upturn towards the second half of 1787, and terminating by the end of 1788. Especially hard hit were the fishing and fur trade, some of the merchants of New England, and the majority of the farmers and planters. This does not exclude the fact that during these years there was a significant increase in manufacturing; nor that certain forms of international trade sprang ahead, as with the Scandinavian countries, Prussia, Russia, the non-British West Indies, and, especially, with the Orient.

Generally speaking, too, as Robert A. East was the first to point out, "the tendency of the hard times [in this period] was to weed out the smaller business men to the eventual benefit of the larger, and to evolve more highly organized business communities; all of which cleared the way for greater business activity in the later years." In this respect, the depression of the 1780s was normal for the capitalist cycle.

Merrill Jensen summarized his views on the question of economic conditions during the Confederacy in these words:

> There is nothing in the knowable facts to support the ancient myth of idle ships, stagnant commerce, and bankrupt merchants in the new nation. As long ago as 1912, Edward Channing demonstrated with adequate evidence that despite the commercial depression, American commerce expanded rapidly after 1783, and that by 1790 the United States had far outstripped the colonies of a few short years before. The evidence of the growth in the amount of commodities exported, and of the tonnage of American ships, shows that not only did Americans regain much of their old commerce, but that they increased it over the dreams of merchants in 1775. Their ships were larger and more numerous; their cargoes were greater in quantity and variety; the whole world was now a market and source of supply.

One fears that in such a summary, the fact that, as Jensen himself wrote, there was a "commercial depression" becomes lost in the extended references to the advances nevertheless made and to conditions which existed by 1790. The fact is that there *was* a commercial depression and an even more profound agricultural depression, and that, since both ended by about 1787, the figures for 1790 do show a considerable advance over comparable figures for 1775.

The reference, moreover, to the writing of Edward Channing is not fully reflective of the content of what that distinguished scholar reported. As concerns the years from the end of the fighting up to the end of the Confederation (not to 1790), here is what Channing wrote in the third volume (pp. 408–09) of his *History of the United States*:

> Once independent and free, the thirteen States found themselves face to face with the commercial barriers of France, Spain and Great Britain. It was one thing to encourage rebellious colonists against an ancient rival; to continue to give them commercial privileges, after their usefulness was gone, was quite another. The French government annulled its decrees giving Americans peculiar rights; Spain closed many ports to their shipping; and the navigation system of Great Britain automatically excluded them from the commerce of the empire. The British government went so far in relaxation as to admit unmanufactured American products to ports of Great Britain, without paying any alien duty, even when brought in American ships; but they closed the trade of the West Indian sugar plantations to American vessels absolutely, although they permitted the lumber and breadstuffs of the continent to be imported in British bottoms. This permission did not extend to salted meats and fish, for this would interfere with the commerce of Nova Scotia, Quebec, Newfoundland, and Ireland. Instead of enjoying freedom of trade with the rest of the world, therefore, American shipowners and producers found themselves cut off by law from some of the most profitable commercial activities of colonial days. Three years of hard times followed and it was not until 1786 that the outlook began to brighten.

Further along, Channing added (p.481): "Statistics that are accessible to us, but were unattainable by the voters in 1786 and 1787, demonstrate the truth of the theory that commercially and industrially the country had regained its prosperity by 1788 and was on the high road to it in 1786."

Very much the same point had been made many years earlier,

in 1871, by Henry B. Dawson; it was made, also, at about the same time as Channing, by Charles A. Beard in his *Economic Interpretation of the Constitution* (1913). Certainly the data are accurately presented and fairly summarized in the sentences quoted from Channing; they demonstrate both the existence of severe depression for several years in the 1780s and the termination of that depression just before the adoption of the Constitution. The latter fact demonstrates that the source of the "critical period" did not lie in the admitted deficiencies of the Articles; they lay rather in the inimitable and immutable features of a capitalist economy, and were to recur from the 1780s on throughout United States history. Nor is there any doubt, as had already been indicated, that the severity of the "critical period" has been exaggerated; yet, for many, conditions were bad enough.

Robert J. Taylor, in his study of *Western Massachusetts in the Revolution* (1954) shows the precipitous fall in farm prices that afflicted the farmers, which, together with a scarcity of money and very high taxes created widespread suffering. Richard P. McCormick, in his examination of the period in New Jersey, reaches similar findings. E. Wilder Spaulding's *New York in the Critical Period* (1932), which is quite critical of the Fiske interpretations, does state (p.18): "Economic depression set in with a vengeance by the end of 1784, giving the state three or four years of gloom, gloom which had begun to disappear only by 1787."

Where the evidence is so overwhelming, only a minimum of specific data are needed. Thus, in the valley counties of Virginia, where, so soon after the Revolution, large plantations based on slavery had not yet secured domination, one finds an enormous number of foreclosures among middling farmers, and hundreds of executions directed against property accumulated only after much labor. In Berkeley County, for example, the number of executions reached 457 by 1784 and came to the staggering total of 945, four years later; in Botetourt, for the same period, the figures rose from 321 to 742. In scores of cases, the sheriffs reported that the execution of the law had been impeded by officers being "kept off by force of arms."

Moving from Virginia, then the most populous State, to Massachusetts, then second to Virginia, one finds the same story of deep suffering. Thus, in Worcester County alone, during the single year 1785–86, there were four thousand suits for debt. Richard B. Morris has written of this area:

> Unable to pay for seed and stock and tools, farmers were thrown into jail or sold out to service. Except for the clothes on the debtor's back, no property was exempt from seizure or execution. There was no homestead exemption, and property at execution sales brought nothing approaching its real value . . . But imprisonment for debt is only part of the story. The records disclose case after case of debtors sold off for sizable terms to work off their debts to their creditors—peonage lacking only the Mexican title.

There were certain features of the commercial and financial life of the nation, under the Confederation, which seemed, to the businessmen and speculators of the time, to impede economic recovery. Probably their total impact was not great, and in several cases, imbalances were in process of correction under the Articles. No doubt, too, those seeking a strongly centralized government for conservative or reactionary political purposes exaggerated the difficulties. Certainly, conditions existed inimical to the fullest and most rapid development of capitalist enterprise.

Robert Morris, a wealthy Philadelphia merchant, appointed Superintendent of Finance by Congress in 1781, when inflation had originated the phrase, "not worth a continental," attempted both the establishment of a national bank and the funding of the national debt as a means of reestablishing the credit of the government, enriching those already rich, and enhancing the strength of the central government. The bank, supported by public funds though directed by private interests, was chartered and lasted several years. As for funding the debt—which, Morris urged in 1782, "will prove the strongest cement to keep the Confederacy together"—this he and his supporters could not accomplish. The failure resulted from the fear that it would not only strengthen the central government, but would significantly alter its character.

The similarity of the Morris program to that put forth by

Hamilton almost a decade later testifies to the continuance of the problems provoking the program and the class interests standing to be served by it.

Actually, there was a notable degree of state assumption of the Federal debt prior to the ratification of the Constitution; this process of liquidating the debt was well advanced by 1788. Indeed, the most thorough student of the question, E. James Ferguson, concluded that had the process "continued a few years longer the federal debt would probably have ceased to exist and the most pressing problem of the Confederation would have been solved without changing the federal system." Possibly, the successful handling of certain key problems helps account for some of the haste with which the Articles of Confederation was discarded.

Another of the failures almost always ascribed to the Articles was the absence of a uniform system of custom duties. Here, too, while some truth adheres to the charge, it has been quite exaggerated; actually notable progress was being made, under the Confederation, towards establishing the necessary uniformity.

Recent research very much modified the traditional Fiske approach. "One of the most noticeable developments before the establishment of of the constitutional government in 1789," such a study found, "was the fact that the States were cooperating to unify their tariff systems and to admit the goods produced or manufactured in the United States duty free."

Its conclusion was: "By 1789 variations in rates and systems was the exception rather than the rule." Of course, to this is to be added the fact that there *were* exceptions; there did persist certain interstate rivalries and provincial restrictions. Furthermore, there was nothing in the Articles which made certain that the trend toward uniformity might not be reversed, rather than completed and made permanent.

The absence of a national currency based upon a generally recognized unit was a severe handicap for economic activity in a commodity market. Early in the Revolution, the Congress adopted the Spanish milled dollar as a standard, and within each State the pound also was standard. To add to the difficulties, the pound had different values in different States. Thus the Georgia pound had 1547 silver grains, that of Virginia, 1289, of New Jersey, 1031, and that of New York but 936. All sorts of coins circulated—dollars, doubloons, johannes, moidores—and business was not stimulated by the fact that a dollar in Virginia amounted to six shillings, while in Maryland it was seven shillings, six pence, and in South Carolina, four shillings, eight pence.

Here, too, however, necessary changes were being made under the Articles, for while they declared that money might be coined either by the Union or by the States, they gave to Congress alone the authority to regulate its value. As a result, under Congress' direction, Jefferson produced in 1784 his "Notes on the Establishment of a Money Unit and of a Coinage for the United States"; following his suggestions, Congress, the next year, accepted the decimal system with the dollar as a basis. Actually a contract was entered into for copper coinage, but the establishment of a mint was not accomplished within the lifetime of the Confederation. Still, the basis for this necessary reform, carried through under the Constitution, was laid under the Articles of Confederation.

More troublesome to the moneyed classes than any of the difficulties already touched upon, was the fact that in seven States, the governments were captured by popular parties and that legislation reflecting this began to appear by the mid-1780s. As a result, inflationary measures aimed at relieving debtors became common as did various stay laws, and moratorium regulations having the same purpose. Sanctity of contract itself, if not the sacredness of private property, seemed to be challenged.

Where such political triumphs and legal reforms were not found to be possible, the aggrieved farmers and poorer folk did not hesitate to adopt drastic mass actions ranging from the forcible barring of sheriff's sales, to organized attacks upon leading governmental officials or institutions. Disorders of a more or less extensive and organized character (beginning in 1782) occurred in Vermont, New Hampshire, Maine (then part of Massachusetts), New York, New Jersey, Virginia and, particularly, in Massachusetts. These were provoked by heavy debts, interest rates that ranged from 25 percent to 40 percent per year, taxation systems that discriminated against the poor, constitutions (especially that of 1780 in Massachusetts) which explicitly favored the rich, foreclosures and sheriffs' sales and imprisonment for debt—in a word by hard times and political grievances that mocked the promises of the just-concluded Revolution.

In New Hampshire, many hundreds gathered at the legislature demanding relief and shouting: "Release us from taxes!" "An End to Debts!" In Maine conventions were held aiming at severance from merchant-dominated Massachusetts. In Virginia, under the leadership of one called Black Matthew, perhaps as many as two hundred men banded together, with arms, refused to pay taxes or debts and swore to resist by force the taking of property for the payment of debts. Most widespread and significant was the rebellion led by the Revolutionary veteran Captain Daniel Shays in western Massachusetts late in 1786 and early in 1787. Said one of the delegates to the people's conventions that appeared through the area:

> . . . the great men are going to get all we have, and I think it is time for us to rise and put a stop to it, and have no more courts, nor sheriffs, nor collectors, nor lawyers, and I know that we are the biggest party, let them say what they will.

In the suppression of the Shays movement, the Federal government came to the assistance of the State; and the rich easterners contributed large sums of money, and their own persons, for the crushing of the effort. There is considerable evidence—tenuous, but still impressive—demonstrating that provocateurs were not missing from this movement and that the Right exaggerated its violent nature, the more decisively to crush it and the better to make political capital out of it. Certainly, the outbreak did intensify the drive from the Right to alter basically the decentralized nature of the Federal government.

The popular nature of the Shays movement was shown not only in the large numbers who joined it; it was shown more decisively in the fact that in the ensuing election the governor responsible for its suppression was retired, permanently, from politics, and the legislature returned was one more amenable to the demands of the debtors than was true before. Such political results also stimulated the efforts to curb the power of the State governments and to enhance that of the national one.

With the Shays outbreak and its suppression one moves into the immediate preparatory stages culminating in the meeting of the Constitutional Convention. Before tracing these stages, it may be useful to summarize some of the main conclusions about the period of the Confederation.

During the period, economic depression was widespread and characteristic, especially among the farmers and the planters. The low point was reached by the end of 1785; recovery had appeared by 1787. It is clear that it was not the Articles which brought about depression; one has, rather, a profit-making economy, which, following a war, went through the normal cycle of inflation, speculation, crisis, hard times and gradual recovery. Thus, the responsibility did not run from the Articles to the depression; if anything, it ran from the depression to the elimination of the Articles.

Under the Articles, a national government was continued, certain essential administrative steps were taken, a land policy of momentous consequences was established, and progress was made in respect to the debt, the commercial interdependence of the States, the development of a national trading policy, and of a national currency system.

Nevertheless, clear evidences of inadequacies were present and were recognized by all elements of the revolutionary coalition, from Left to Right; to this as a basic source of the movement to strengthen the central government is to be added the growth of a national consciousness, which also was not confined to any political spectrum, nor to any particular class.

At the same time, there was, ever since the mid-1770s, a slow rightward drift in the balance of the Revolution. Given the basic nature of that Revolution as bourgeois-democratic, and given the hegemony of the bourgeoisie in its conduct, and the signifi- cant presence of slavery, it was natural that this drift developed as the Revolution advanced and then as its success became apparent. It was natural too, that with success such a drift should even be intensified.

Hence, undoubtedly, in the efforts at greater centralization, culminating in the holding of the Constitutional Convention, there is a strong Right ingredient. Yet, it must be emphasized again, this is not at all the entire or even the main component of the movement resulting in the Constitution. The main thing is the effort to consolidate the bourgeois-democratic revolution and to assure the permanence of its major results.[2] Behind this stood the majority of the forces which made the Revolution, although significant and varying degrees of opposition developed from elements within the Left and the Right, and from the entire far Right which had always stood opposed to the Revolution itself.

Chapter III

The Movement for a New Constitution

Proposals of a more or less specific character for the strengthening of the Federal government were quite common, beginning about 1780. It is difficult and somewhat arbitrary to fasten on any one as marking clearly the beginning of a continuous line of proposals and actions that terminate with the Philadelphia Convention of May, 1787. But one that is as good as another is the act of the Massachusetts legislature (and also of New Hampshire) in June, 1785 attempting the regulation of trade and commerce. This act resulted from the absence of any restrictions against importation of British goods into the United States which led, by 1784–85, to a practical monopoly of trade in major cities by British merchants. Furthermore, this resulted in the swift disappearance of hard money into the hands of the British competitors just when various State legislatures were in the midst of inflationary programs.

In addition to the commercial regulatory act, the Massachusetts legislature instructed the State's delegates to the Congress to press for "a *well-guarded* power to regulate the trade of the United States." Though the emphasis was in the original resolution, the Massachusetts delegation refused to act in accordance therewith, explaining to the Governor in September, 1785, that they feared it might serve as a pretext for the formation of a convention which would seek to act not only on trade, but to "revise the Confederation *generally*." Plans were on foot, said these delegates, to establish

> baleful aristocracies . . . We are apprehensive and it is our duty to declare it, that such a measure would produce throughout the Union, an exertion by friends of an aristocracy, to send members who would promote a change of government . . . "more power in Congress" has been the cry from all quarters . . . We are for increasing the power of Congress, as far as it will promote the happiness of the people; but at the same time are clearly of opinion that every measure should be avoided which would strengthen the hands of the enemies to a free government.

Shortly thereafter (January, 1786) problems arising out of an absence of a national trade and commercial policy led the Virginia legislature to propose the holding of an interstate commercial convention to meet in Annapolis. Four States—Georgia, South Carolina, Connecticut, and, rather ironically, Maryland—took no action on this invitation, but nine did select delegates. The delegates, however, from New Hampshire, Massachusetts, Rhode Island, and North Carolina failed to arrive in time to participate, so that only the delegates from New York, New Jersey, Pennsylvania, Delaware, and Virginia were present.

Since only a minority of the States were present, the delegates felt that no significant accomplishment was possible. They agreed, therefore, to issue a call for another convention, having wider scope, to meet on the second Monday of May, 1787 in Philadelphia. To draft this call, the delegates chose Alexander Hamilton. On September 14, 1786, the Annapolis Convention approved and forwarded it to Congress; there it was urged that the delegates to the projected Convention consider not only commercial matters, but proceed

> to take into consideration the situation of the United States, to devise such further provisions as shall appear to them necessary to render the Constitution of the Federal Government adequate to the exigencies of the Union; and to report such an act for that purpose to the United States in Congress assembled, as when agreed to, by them, and afterwards confirmed by the Legislature of every State, will effectually provide for the same . . .

There is some evidence that the organizers of the Annapolis Convention anticipated the poor attendance from which it suffered; also it appears that at least some among them conceived of using the failure of the Annapolis meeting as a springboard for projecting another and more comprehensive gathering in the future. Thus it is that Madison wrote to Jefferson, in August, 1786:

> Many Gentlemen both within & without Congress wish to make this [Annapolis] meeting subservient to a plenipotentiary Convention for amending the Confederation. Though my wishes are in favor of such an event; yet I despair so much of its accomplishment at the present crisis that I do not extend my views beyond a commercial reform. To speak the truth I almost despair even of this.

More revealing is a letter written October 10, 1786, by Louis Otto, the French *charge d'affaires* to Vergennes, his Foreign Minister, evaluating the Annapolis development:

> Although there are no nobles in America, there is a class of men denominated "gentlemen," . . . and although many of these men have betrayed the interests of their order to gain popularity, there reigns among them a connection so much more intimate as they almost all of them dread the efforts of the people to despoil them of their possessions, and, moreover, they are creditors, and therefore interested in strengthening the government, and watching over the execution of the law . . . The majority of them being merchants, it is for their interest to establish the credit of the United States in Europe on a solid foundation by the exact payment of debts, and to grant to Congress powers extensive enough to compel the people to contribute for this purpose.

Otto went on to explain that "for a very long time . . . the necessity of imparting to the Federal government more energy and vigor has been felt," but, he added that it was also felt that the liberties of individuals under their State governments and the relative independence of the State governments from the central one, were very dear to the American people. Hence to make changes in such a system one had to proceed "with great precautions."

It was widely believed, continued the French observer, that strengthening the central government would lead to "a marked preponderance of rich men and of large proprietors" and this belief made popular suspicions all the greater.

As for the Annapolis meeting in particular, Otto wrote: " . . . the commissioners were unwilling to take into consideration the grievances of commerce, which are of exceeding interest for the people, without at the same time perfecting the fundamental constitution of Congress."

Meanwhile, for several months, the question of a more or less basic reform in the government had been debated within Congress itself. A precipitant of this debate was New Jersey's flat refusal, in February, 1786, to pay its share of the requisitions called for by Congress in the fall of 1785. Early in May, 1786, Charles Pinckney of South Carolina moved in Congress for a thorough reorganization of the government. In June, Congress debated the Pinckney motion; the result was a series of proposed amendments submitted in August by a special committee. These amendments aimed to enhance the judicial powers of the Federal government, to ensure Congressional control over foreign and interstate commerce, and to greatly strengthen the capacity of the Confederacy to enforce its requisitions upon the States. Congress, however, never submitted these suggested amendments to the States, apparently despairing of ever getting the unanimous vote required.

Then, in September, 1786, Congress was presented with the Hamilton paper from the Annapolis Convention. It referred this to a committee in October and finally endorsed the proposal, in guarded terms, on February 21, 1787. Prior to this action, and in part spurring it on, six States (Georgia, Delaware, North Carolina, Pennsylvania, Virginia, and New Jersey), acting on their own responsibility, had already appointed delegates to meet in Philadelphia for the purpose of amending the Articles.

Congress, however, being the only body authorized to initiate such amendments, finally acted, at New York's suggestion, on the date stated above, thus giving official sanction to the forthcoming Philadelphia Convention. It did so in these words:

> Whereas there is provision in the Articles of Confederation and perpetual union, for making alterations therein . . . And whereas

experience hath evinced, that there are defects in the present Confederation, as a means to remedy which, several of the States . . . have suggested a convention for the purposes expressed in the following Resolution . . .

Resolved, That in the opinion of Congress, it is expedient, that on the second Monday in May next [May 14], a Convention of Delegates who shall have been appointed by the several States, be held at Philadelphia, for the sole and express purpose of revising the Articles of Confederation, and reporting to Congress and the several Legislatures, such alterations and provisions therein, as shall, when agreed to in Congress, and confirmed by the States, render the federal constitution adequate to the exigencies of Government, and the preservation of the Union.

Thereafter, and prior to May 14, New York, South Carolina, Massachusetts, Connecticut and Maryland selected delegates. New Hampshire did not do so until June (her delegates did not reach Philadelphia until July 23); Rhode Island, whose government was firmly in the hands of an anti-creditor party, never did participate in the Constitutional Convention.

Such were the sources, background, method of selecting delegates, authority and avowed intention of the convention of "demi-gods"—to use Jefferson's description—which met in Philadelphia in the spring and summer of 1787.

• • •

To summarize: the movement towards a stronger central government which resulted in the Constitution, sprang fundamentally from the desire of the propertied elements for a stable government sensitive to their requirements, and their need for a unified, manageable national market which they could exploit and develop and on the basis of which they could themselves expand. These basic drives merged with the wider national feeling of the people, in turn intensified by the very real drawback a loosely federated union represented in terms of foreign affairs. Present, especially on the Right, was the desire to capitalize on the movement for greater unity by making that newly unified government as little responsive as possible to popular pressure, and to make it not only an instrument for the enrichment of the few but also an instrument, when necessary, for the vigorous repression of mass activity, from the unfree as well as the free. On the other hand, however, powerful elements on the extreme Right wanted to destroy the Republic and replace it with either a single monarchy or with several confederations more or less closely dependent upon Great Britain. Part of the urge for stronger centralization was directed towards the preservation of what democratic advance had been made, and the maintenance of what was then the greatest beacon-light of republican, popular government.[1]

Chapter IV

The Constitution: Basic Facts

WHILE NEARLY everything about the Constitution of the United States has been and remains a matter of debate, there are certain basic facts about its history which are not controversial and knowledge of which is essential.

On the date set by Congress for the opening of the Convention—May 14, 1787—only the delegates from Pennsylvania and Virginia had arrived at the State House in Philadelphia (the present Independence Hall). These, and others as they arrived, met from day to day and, finding no quorum, adjourned, until, on May 25, it was found that delegates from seven of the States—a majority—had arrived. Having then a quorum, the Convention formally opened.

The twenty-nine delegates then present began the activities of the Convention with the election of a presiding officer; Robert Morris of Pennsylvania nominated George Washington. This most revered figure in the country was approved unanimously.

A total of seventy-four delegates had been selected by twelve States; some declined the honor and some failed to attend for other reasons. The total number of actual delegates in attendance at any time came to fifty-five. The final draft of the Constitution was presented for the delegates' vote on September 17; the delegations from all twelve States voted in favor. At this time, present to vote were forty-two delegates, and of these, thirty-nine voted affirmatively; three—Elbridge Gerry of Massachusetts, George Mason of Virginia and Edmund Randolph of Virginia—voted negatively.

The negative vote was this minute because other opponents of the draft—among them, Luther Martin of Maryland, John Lansing and Robert Yates of New York—had left earlier. Still, the delegations as a whole voted in every case in favor; this made true the style with which the Draft was submitted—at Franklin's urging—to the country: "Done in Convention by the Unanimous Consent of the States present."

Exactly how to forward the Draft was perplexing. The Convention had decided that it was to be submitted to State conventions for ratification or rejection, but should this be done with no consideration at all of the existing, though feeble, Congress? It had been of some consequence that Congress had authorized, belatedly, the meeting of the Philadelphia Convention. This Convention, instead of amending the Articles as empowered by Congress had drafted an entirely new document; it had provided that the Draft be approved not by Congress but by popular ratification expressed through specially elected state conventions; and it had provided that the ratification be considered in effect not when all the States had agreed (as required by the Articles), but when only nine of them had done so.

This was irregularity—not to say, illegality—enough; should it be further compounded by ignoring Congress altogether in the act of submitting the Draft to the test of ratification? The problem was resolved by having the President forward the Draft to Congress, with the request that that body then submit it to the States for action.

In Congress, a debate raged as to how to receive the Draft, and what to do with it. The controversy finally simmered down to two alternatives: one side pressed for the submission of the Draft with no recommendation of approval or disapproval, but accompanied by suggested amendments (including provision for a Bill of Rights); the other side pressed for submission of the Draft to the States without any suggested amendments and with an expression of approval.

The controversy was resolved by agreement that the Draft would be submitted, with no one voting negatively, in its original form, without amendments. The Congress, then, did throw the mantle of legality over the series of illegalities committed by the Convention, for it approved the submission of the document to the States for final determination by their own Conventions.[1]

The Congress in thus approving what amounted to an ignoring of its own sovereignty was acknowledging its own actual impotence. For several months in 1786–1787, in fact, the Congress had not had enough members in attendance for a quorum; in the fall of 1788 it failed again to muster a quorum. In the spring of 1789, with the new government coming into being, the Congress of the Confederation passed out of existence; two members were present at the funeral. The fact is that for six months prior to the formal interment, there had been actually no government of the United States.

We may conclude this brief presentation of the bare factual framework relative to the Constitution with a table presenting the data on its ratification:

Ratification of the United States Constitution

(Took effect June 21, 1788, when New Hampshire, the ninth state, ratified.)

| STATE | DATE | VOTE | |
		YES	NO
1. Del.	12/7/87	Unanimous	
2. Pa.	12/12/87	46	23
3. N.J.	12/18/87	Unanimous	
4. Ga.	1/2/88	Unanimous	
5. Conn.	1/9/88	128	40
6. Mass.	2/6/88	187	168
7. Md.	4/20/88	63	11
8. S.C.	5/23/88	149	73
9. N.H.	6/21/88	57	46
10. Va.	6/25/88	89	79
11. N.Y.	7/26/88	30	27
12. N.C.	11/21/89	195	77
13. R.I.	5/29/90	34	32

When one moves away from factual chronicling to analysis and evaluation, he enters at once into the area of debate and controversy. This controversy has developed a significance of its own, second only to that of the document itself. Let us turn, then, to an analysis of the Constitution, paying attention to the nature of contrary or divergent views.

• • •

For over half a century, two apparently contrasting views of the United States Constitution have been competing for approval. These are conveniently summarized in the preface to a volume in the *Amherst Readings in Problems in American Civilization,* a series widely used in institutions of higher learning. Earl Latham, editor of the volume on *The Declaration of Independence and the Constitution* (1949), asks:

> What was it the Founding Fathers did in Philadelphia in 1787? Were they selfless patriots bent upon establishing a new and enduring form of government . . . Or were they self-seekers bent instead upon protecting the material advantages of the propertied class . . . ?

These alternatives—which may be labeled (with not quite complete accuracy) the pre- and post-Beardian views—by no means exhaust the possible opinions one may have of the Constitution; nor are they basically contrasting *as to the nature of the Constitution itself.* Whether one depicts the Constitution as the divinely-inspired document described in some elementary textbooks or in the speeches of American Legion and Daughters of American Revolution (D.A.R.) functionaries, or as the product of very practical, rich, supremely competent politicians, does not mean that the document itself need differ. On the contrary, is not a "practical," rich politician the D.A.R.'s idea of a divine instrumentality?

The fact is that, *as to substance,* the pre- and post-Beardian views of the Constitution hardly differ. The Beard view (classically formulated in his *Economic Interpretation of the Constitution,* first published in 1913) presented the document as an ultraconservative one, contemptuous of democratic rights, and devoted to the sanctification and protection of the rich minority.

This view was not at all new.[2] On the contrary, Beard himself had earlier said substantially the same thing, as in the preface to his *Readings in American Government and Politics* (1909), and particularly in his *The Supreme Court and the Constitution* (1912).

It was the view insisted upon by the Federalists from Fisher

Ames to Alexander Hamilton in their struggle against the Jeffersonians; it was the view of the slaveholders from Robert Hayne to Jefferson Davis, advanced in their effort to preserve slavery and then to justify secession. It was the view vigorously argued at the end of the nineteenth and the beginning of the twentieth centuries by partisans of rising monopolies—the view, for example, urged on the Supreme Court by Joseph Choate in the income tax case (1894) and adopted by that Court to vindicate its reactionary decisions of that period—in that case, the antitrust cases and the labor injunction cases.

It is the view present in the writings of professional and eminently conservative historians of that period, as George Bancroft, John W. Burgess, Samuel B. Harding, John Bach McMaster—Burgess going so far as to refer to the adoption of the Constitution in terms of a *coup d'etat*. Publicists of the Wilson, Theodore Roosevelt, La Follette brand of liberalism took the same position; an example is J. Allen Smith's *The Spirit of American Government* (1907), the third chapter of which is entitled, "The Constitution a Reactionary Government." Early socialist books, more economic determinist than Marxist, did not differ on this point, as the writings of A.M. Simons, Gustavus Myers, and Allan L. Benson attest; the last named entitled one of his books, published in 1913, *Our Dishonest Constitution*. Somewhat later, Arthur W. Calhoun, writing in the same tradition, felt it important that it be "made perfectly clear that the United States Constitution was made by a conspiracy of business interests hostile to democracy."

The New Deal view, as the earlier New Freedom view, held to this same estimate of the Constitution's quality. A typical example of this is J. W. Jacobson's, *The Development of American Political Thought* (1932); in the chapter on "Writing the National Constitution," that document is presented as the culmination of a Right-wing movement away from the spirit and content of the Declaration of Independence—"No movement in world history is . . . a more complete rebound of the pendulum," permeated as it allegedly was, in contrast to the Declaration, with "the uniform distrust on democracy."

This view of the Constitution's substance still prevails quite widely. Representative is the treatment in one of the more liberal college textbooks, by three professors, Ray A. Billington, Bert J. Loewenberg and Samuel J. Brockunier. There the Constitution is presented as the culmination of a "conservative reaction" and the reader is told that at its drafting, "the great Revolutionary liberals—Thomas Jefferson, Sam Adams, John Hancock, Patrick Henry—were not there; the propertied legislators no longer trusted them."[3] A political science textbook by a university professor and a State Department official assured its readers that the character of the Constitution "was determined to a great extent by men who wanted to make America safe against democracy." A distinguished attorney, Leo Pfeffer, associate general counsel of the American Jewish Congress, presented the Constitution as quite literally the result of conspirators operating deliberately and secretly in violation of the law. At its drafting, once more, the reader is told that "the radicals were conspicuously absent," and the same list of absentees is presented, and as to substance, this is what one gets: "The principal if not sole purpose of this strong, central government was to protect men of substance from the predatory designs of the populace."

If there has been and remains—with some exceptions, to be discussed later—this near-unanimity, it may well be asked: why the furor over Beard's *Economic Interpretation of the Constitution?* For furor there was, with most (not all) of respectability, from the *New York Times* to Nicholas Murray Butler, then President of Columbia University, denouncing the volume as little short of obscene.

The full answer does not lie in a misreading of Beard's intent as one seeking to discredit the Constitution, though such misreading did occur and still persists.[4] What *was* new in Beard's work and was disturbing to partisans of the status quo was not Beard's insistence on the reactionary nature of the Constitution (why should that bother them?) but rather his attempted detailed demonstration that the Constitution had the character hitherto ascribed to it not because this represented eternal verity, but rather because it represented the class needs and desires of its framers.

Beard repeatedly and pointedly emphasized this in the volume. Thus, a few examples:

> The Concept of the Constitution as a piece of abstract legislation reflecting no group interests and recognizing no economic antagonisms is entirely false.

Again, somewhat more sharply, he insisted that the political leaders of the eighteenth century,

> were not under the necessity of obscuring—at least to the same extent as modern partisan writers—the essential economic antagonisms featuring in law and constitution making (p.189).

And, even more sharply, Beard wrote that then it was

> unnecessary for political writers to address themselves to the proletariat and to explain dominant group interests in such manner as to make them appear in the garb of "public policy."

It was this insistence (partial though it was) upon the class nature of the law and of the state which was obscene to President Butler and the *Times,* exactly because it unquestionably was a contribution to realistic and critical thinking about United States history and society.[5]

Nevertheless, it must again be pointed out that Beard's volume did not contradict, but rather confirmed, the view hitherto generally held and insisted upon, especially by the Right, as to the nature and the substance of the Constitution itself. This Right, however, had maintained that the Constitution was what the Right said it was because *that* was the only reasonable, decent, practical, sound and publicly useful character that existed—all else was wrong-headed at best and "communistic" at worst. Was it erroneous only in the latter, and not in its estimate of the nature, the substance, of the Constitution itself?

Was the Constitution the product of reactionary and counter-revolutionary forces as has been stated from Burgess to Beard to Jensen?[6] Was it the reactionary document the Federalists, the slaveholders and more recently the monopolists insisted it was for reasons both obvious and weighty?

We may begin our analysis of this question by returning to the typical statement already quoted from the Billington-

Loewenberg-Brockunier textbook: "The great Revolutionary liberals—Thomas Jefferson, Sam Adams, John Hancock, Patrick Henry—were not there at the Constitutional Convention; the propertied legislators no longer trusted them."

This clearly conveys the impression that all the gentlemen named were not only absent from the Convention, but were opposed to its work (and presumably therefore were absent); that, unlike those who were present, these gentlemen were not especially "propertied"; and that those who were "propertied" no longer trusted them. In each of these particulars, the truth is otherwise.

That "evidence" of this kind should be offered repeatedly to establish the idea of the Constitution as a reactionary document is itself sufficient, when the facts are known, to cast serious doubts on that idea.

The list of those missing from the Convention might well be expanded. For example, John Adams also was not present, but presumably he was not one of "the great Revolutionary liberals," so that his absence (as Minister to Great Britain) would not support the thesis. And, of course, John Adams supported the Constitution.

But then Thomas Jefferson, one of the key absentees and one of the "distrusted" ones, was absent because he was the Minister to France, having been appointed in 1785 to succeed Benjamin Franklin in this key diplomatic post—a strange demonstration of distrust. Furthermore, Jefferson did not oppose the Constitution but rather, on the whole, supported it from the first moment that he read it, and his support for it grew as he pondered the document and the circumstances bringing it forth. Furthermore, in terms of the "distrust" of propertied elements, when Jefferson returned from his Paris post, in 1789, he was immediately appointed Secretary of State by President Washington!

John Hancock, another of the "distrusted" ones, was Governor of Massachusetts from 1780 to 1785, and President of the Congress from 1785 to 1786, when illness forced him to resign. Hancock was the presiding officer in the Massachusetts Convention of 1788 which ratified the Constitution, an act accomplished with Hancock's support. "Distrust" for Hancock was further manifested in his election as Governor again from 1787 to 1793.

Samuel Adams, who had in 1779, helped frame the Massachusetts Constitution, served in the Congress until 1781, and was a member of the Massachusetts Convention in 1788 which ratified the Constitution, and he also voted for ratification.

Only Patrick Henry, of those mentioned as being absent, opposed the ratification of the Constitution—a matter to be examined later. But Henry's absence was not due to "distrust" on the part of "propertied" elements; it was due to his own will, for Henry had been selected as a delegate to the Convention and refused to attend. His position as Governor of Virginia, in 1784–86 (for the fifth time) also would appear not to support the idea that propertied elements distrusted him. (As a matter of fact, Henry dominated the very propertied legislature of Virginia and so kept his political enemy, James Madison, the father of the Constitution, from being selected as a Senator after the Constitution was ratified).

This examination might be extended to include another of the radical leaders whose absence from the Convention is often pointed to as further evidence of its reactionary and sinister purposes—namely, Thomas Paine. He, like Jefferson, was abroad; however, he like Jefferson, supported ratification of the Constitution, though there were features of it which he, like Samuel Adams and Jefferson (and John Adams, and Alexander Hamilton, for that matter) disapproved. But, as he wrote Washington, in 1796; "I would have voted for it myself, had I been in America, or even for worse, rather than have had none . . . ."

Thomas Jefferson approved the holding of the Constitutional Convention and said, after he had learned of its personnel: "We may be assured their propositions will be wise, as a more able assembly never sat in America." When the document appeared, Jefferson declared, "I approved, from the first, of the great mass of what is in the new Constitution." Yet, on further study, it is true, while he saw "a great mass of good in it, in a very desirable form," still "there is also to me a bitter pill or two," and so he then thought of himself as "nearly a Neutral."

The "bitter pills" were an absence of a Bill of Rights and the possibility of permanent tenure for the President, but the fact is that upon the ratification of the Constitution, Jefferson said he felt "infinite pleasure." To his closest friend and most influential member of the Constitutional Convention, James Madison, Jefferson wrote, July 31, 1788:

> I sincerely rejoice at the acceptance of our new constitution by nine states [the number needed to give it effect]. It is a good canvas, on which some strokes only want retouching. What these are, I think are sufficiently manifested by the general voice from North and South, which calls for a bill of rights.

Meanwhile, across the waters, pro-monarchical writers had been describing anarchy in the republican United States. They dismissed the idea of republican unity and stability for the United States as "the idlest and most visionary of notions." On the other hand, the Constitution and its ratification were hailed by "Scottish Burgh reformer, Irish patriot, British radical" as a "thorn in the flesh" of tyrants, monarchs and their sycophants.

To treat as a reactionary document, an ultraconservative triumph, a defeat for democracy, a counterrevolutionary coup, this document hailed at the time by radicals and revolutionists in Europe, one for whose ratification Samuel Adams and John Hancock voted, one for which Thomas Paine said he would have voted, and one whose ratification made Thomas Jefferson "sincerely rejoice" is, to say the least, paradoxical. It is, in fact, to misinterpret the Constitution, to view it partially, mechanically and divorced from its time and place.

Chapter V

The Political Theory of the Constitution

THE CONSTITUTION of the United States, as originally drafted, was a bourgeois-democratic document for the governing of a slaveholder-capitalist republic. It did not represent a renunciation of the American Revolution, but rather a consolidation of that Revolution by the classes which had led it.

The very idea of a written constitution wherein the powers of government are enumerated represented a logical consummation of that Revolution. Its enumeration in specific and defined form connoted, in the first place, the idea of the scientific nature of politics. The Constitution signified a confirmation of the principles of the Age of Reason in matters of politics. Here, through debate and study, had been drafted and ratified a charter for human government; it was not something to be left to divine will, or the advice of priests or the whims of royalty. Rather, it was to express in the area of government reasonable and tested findings resulting from human experience and study. From that point of view, the Constitution was as scientific and as rational (if not as exact) as Newton's physics.

Furthermore, the idea of a written Constitution having limited and specific powers bestowed upon government reflects the Revolution's insistence which, with Locke and against Hobbes, saw inherent evil in regulation and control—indeed, in government itself. In this sense the movement from the Confederation to the Constitution, which represents a movement toward stronger and more centralized government, does represent a retreat from the viewpoint of the Left in the Revolutionary coalition. Yet, the retreat is partial, and as we have seen, the need for a government stronger than that of the Confederation was felt by all components of the coalition—Hamilton *and* Jefferson, Washington *and* Paine.

The main point is that the heart of liberty, in its bourgeois, antifeudal connotation, is the absence of restraint; it is not the wherewithal, coming from government, to accomplish desired objectives. Hence, where there is tyranny—in the eighteenth century this went under the form of monarchy—there would be and could be no written constitution, since enumerating the powers of the omnipotent is absurd.

This is why to conservatism's leading ideologist, Edmund Burke, a written constitution appeared seditious, *per se*, while to Thomas Paine, as he wrote in his *Rights of Man*, it was "to liberty, what a grammar is to language." For Paine, the presence of a written constitution connoted the opposite of tyranny, i.e., popular sovereignty; therefore, he held that "a government without a constitution is power without right."

Dependence upon reason, rather than authority, was as characteristic of the bourgeois-democratic effort as was the desire for an absence of restraint. Hence, Jefferson wrote, March 18, 1789, not only that he was sure the Constitution "is unquestionably the wisest ever presented to men," but, and particularly, that: "The example of changing a Constitution, by assembling the wise men of the State, instead of assembling armies, will be worth as much to the world as the former examples we had given them."

The dependence upon reason, the desire for an absence of restraint, the opposition to hereditary status and a closed static system reflect capitalism's opposition to feudalism. All this, together with the alleged natural quality of the market, wherefore the need for *laissez faire* in economics, produced a sense of equality. Thus, the employer and the employee come to market and each freely indicates his desires; one for the purchase of labor power and skill, the other for the sale of both. And the price and conditions of the transaction were resolved by the immutable law of supply and demand, a law as natural as the law governing the movement of the planets.

All these considerations together illuminate Engels' remark—in a letter dated March 24, 1884—that "the logical form of bourgeois domination is precisely the democratic republic . . . ."

The feudal emphasis upon tenure and authority makes status the basic aim of society; the bourgeois emphasis upon fluidity, progress and reason makes property the basic aim of society. So, Locke concludes; "The great and chief end, therefore, of men's uniting into commonwealths and putting themselves under government is the preservation of their property." Thus, amongst the delegates at the Constitutional Convention there is very near unanimity[1] on this point. Property, said Gouverneur Morris of New York, is "the main object of Society"; "the principal object," said John Rutledge of South Carolina; "the primary object," said Rufus King of Massachusetts; "the great object," said Pierce Butler of South Carolina; "the primary objects of civil society are the security of property and public safety," said James Madison of Virginia.

This property is to be secured by freedom, i.e., freedom from restraints, delimiting laws, regulatory provisions, and status-enshrined privileges.[2] Property so secured and so freed will thereby be enhanced. The accumulation is the hallmark of freedom and the varied and *unequal distribution of that accumulated property is the result as it is the essence of liberty.* Madison, leading theoretician of the Constitution, repeatedly made that point. Writing to Jefferson, October 24, 1787, he insisted that what he called "natural distinctions"—by which he meant property distinctions as contrasted to "artificial ones" based on religion or politics—"results from the very protection which a free Government gives to unequal facilities of acquiring it." It was characteristic of the severe limitations of even a Madison that distinctions and limitations based upon sex and color did not enter into his consideration—and no doubt never occurred to the recipient of this letter.

As to the male-bias, one is reminded of a woman character in the novel *Alcuyn: A Dialogue on the Rights of Women* (1797), by Charles Brockden Brown, who complains that "lawmakers thought as little of comprehending us in their code of liberty as if we were pigs or sheep."

And as to racism, those people who were of African origin were held to be *naturally* slaves—just as women were held to be *naturally* unequal to and therefore subordinate to men—and so were considered quite literally as property, as pigs or sheep. Those men and women who were called Indians also were considered as naturally out of the ken of "civilized" politics. They went simply unnoticed in the Constitution—as were women—for they were legally held to be of other "nations" and actually felt to be fit only for removal or annihilation. Free Black people also go unconsidered in the Constitution, but slaves, constituting a very considerable proportion of the extant property, had to be mentioned, in terms both of securing their possession and benefiting those who owned them (as in representation apportionment); still it is notable that those drafting the Constitution deliberately refused to use the words *slave* or *slavery*, reflecting embarrassment and, perhaps, the hope that the institution would not last as long as the nation for which the Constitution was being drafted.

When Madison equated freedom with inequality in the Convention, Hamilton eagerly expressed agreement. Said Hamilton, June 26, 1787: "It was certainly true: that nothing like an equality of property existed; that an inequality would exist as long as liberty existed, and that it would unavoidably result from that very liberty itself." He went on to touch upon "the distinction between rich and poor," but bethought himself and said: "He meant not however to enlarge on the subject."

Civilization was a social order in which the private ownership of property was fundamental; those living in civilized societies *naturally* sought to maximize their possession of property. It was exactly because the institution of private property and the desire for individual self-aggrandizement seemed to be absent in the societies of the so-called Indians that they were deemed barbaric or savage.

For basically the same reason, those who could not possess property or who did not succeed in obtaining significant property holdings were outside politics; this included children, women, slaves, Indians, indentured servants and—generally—the poor. Such people were not *in* politics; they were the object of political control. They were problems for statesmen; they required *policing* within the body-politic.

In the famous Tenth number of *The Federalist*, Madison wrote:

> The diversity in the faculties of men, from which the rights of property originate [!], is not less an insuperable obstacle to a uniformity of interests. The protection of these faculties is the first object of government. From the protection of different and unequal faculties of acquiring property, the possession of different degrees and kinds of property immediately results; and from the influence of these on the sentiments and views of the respective proprietors, ensues a division of the society into different interests and parties.

Madison went on to declare that "the latent causes of factions are thus sown in the nature of man" producing different opinions, different attractions; there exists, he thought, a "propensity of mankind to fall into mutual animosities." Perhaps feeling uncomfortable with this rather uncharacteristic descent into mysticism and an almost theological view of "original sin," Madison quickly went on to more material matters:

> But the most common and durable sources of factions has been the various and unequal distribution of property. *Those who hold and those who are without property have ever formed distinct interests in society.* Those who are creditors, and those who are debtors, fall under a like discrimination. A landed interest, a manufacturing interest, a mercantile interest, a moneyed interest, with many lesser interests, grow up of necessity in civilized nations, and divide them into different classes, actuated by different sentiments and views. The regulation of these various and interfering interests forms the principal task of modern legislation, and involves the spirit of party and faction in the necessary and ordinary operations of the government. (italics added–H.A.)

For Madison and his class peers, the underlined sentence is a permanent condition of "civilized society." He conceives of the idea, in this same essay, of "reducing mankind to a perfect equality in their political rights" but an equality of economic rights, i.e., the elimination of the unequal distribution of property or, even more, the elimination of the private ownership of the means of production, would be anarchy and not government, since, as classical political economy insisted, the essential purpose of government was the protection of private property.

Hence, what remains as a prime function of government is the regulation of the differing propertied groups (landed, manufacturing, mercantile, etc.) so that no one of them oppresses or tyrannizes over any of the others.

The Constitution we have drafted, Madison insisted, succeeds in producing a government which will do this. This required ingenuity, compromise and perseverance but it has been accomplished. He and his readers knew that already significant challenges to the political supremacy of the rich had appeared, with movements to abolish debts, to prevent foreclosures, to inflate the currency and even, as in Massachusetts, embodied an armed resistance of thousands of the economically distraught, requiring stern military measures to repress. But with this instrument of government to span our entire nation, with its enormous size and different climates, products and industries:

> A rage for paper money, for an abolition of debts, for an equal division of property, or for any other improper or wicked project, will be less apt to pervade the whole body of the Union than a particular member of it; in the same proportion as such a malady is more likely to taint a particular county or district, than an entire State.

Concluding this Tenth number, then, Madison saw in the Constitution "a republican remedy for the diseases most incident to republican government"; that remedy rested in considerable part on the strength of the union of the States, wherefore we should show "zeal in cherishing the spirit and supporting the character of Federalists."

It is noteworthy that in this essay Madison is affirming the inevitability of parties or factions; this despite the fact that at that time both were in ill repute and held to reflect the decay of tyrannical or monarchical governments. Parties, being a group of like-minded people seeking political power, their formation was long held in Britain to be seditious since there power inhered in the Crown. The factional disputes that marked British politics were often pointed to by the colonists and the Revolutionists in the New World as evidence of extreme corruption. There is no mention of political parties in the Constitution, and Washington always insisted that their existence would threaten or did threaten the viability of a republic. The point in the latter case was that now, in theory, power inhered in the people—"We, the People"—and that, therefore, parties or factions seeking political power were doing so in an effort to seize that power from the people. Hence for a full generation after the Revolution it was always the other group who was forming a party; the group doing the attacking would always claim that it represented no party but rather the nation as a whole. This is why, when Jefferson set about actually creating the party that was to become the lineal ancestor of the present Democratic Party, he did so in utmost secrecy.

So far as political theory in Britain was concerned, the solution to this problem of the existence of parties in fact and their illegality and subversiveness in theory came notably from Edmund Burke who developed the concept of the Loyal Opposition, i.e., there could be parties so long as they agreed that government existed for the protection of property and so long as the Crown itself was not threatened. The British even institutionalized this; thus, Her Majesty's Loyal Opposition is an established part of the governmental structure and two members of Parliament are paid more than ordinary members: the Prime Minister and the leader of that opposition.

In the United States, parties were acceptable and fully legal so long as they represented any of the propertied interests enumerated by Madison (or any combination thereof) and so long as they abided by the Constitution's guarantee of a republican form of government. In both cases, however, it was understood that while there would be, as Madison stated, those with property and those without property and that these "have ever formed distinct interests in society" it is only the former who have a real stake in society and who therefore should govern. Those who own the country should govern it, said John Jay, one of the authors of *The Federalist* papers and to be the first Chief Justice of the United States; but among those who participated in that ownership there were different interests and therefore different factions and parties. Among them, however, was no disagreement on the necessity to keep sacred the rights of private property and the sanctity of contract. A party that did not agree to this basic condition was not a legal party; it was a seditious organization and its members were criminals.

Government existed then to prevent tyranny, i.e., such as the monarchy lately overthrown in a successful revolution. And also to prevent anarchy, agrarianism, levelism or "chaos" when the poor, the "Many-Headed Beast" of Spenser's poetry, threatened to take power into their own hands and thus smash civilization.

The essence of liberty, then, for the possessors of private property, was the liberty to accumulate and securely possess that property. This liberty entailed inequality; it applied to a fraction of the population, naturally, since only a fraction was capable of acquiring the property. That Madison based this liberty and this inequality upon immutable "human nature" indicates that exploiting ruling classes always see their system as immortal—all the lessons of history to the contrary notwithstanding.

The enunciation by those property owners at that time and place and under those circumstances of the sacredness of property rights and the freedom to accumulate capital and to protect the resulting human inequalities, cannot be equated with verbally similar protestations of devotion to "free enterprise" by a present day monopolistic, thoroughly reactionary capitalism. True it is that the limitations and contradictions in the earlier cries of "liberty" are central to an understanding of the corruption that "liberty" can undergo in less than two centuries, but one must not depict the nature of the sturdy ancestor in terms of the foul offspring.

Chapter VI

The Contents of the Constitution

CHARLES A. BEARD concluded the chapter (VI) in his *Economic Interpretation of the Constitution*, dealing with the actual contents of the document itself, with these words:

> It was an economic document drawn with superb skill by men whose property interests were immediately at stake; and as such it appealed directly and unerringly to identical interests in the country at large.

This statement is characteristic of the oversimplification that marks Beard's very influential view. The emphasis on the alleged "immediate" interests of the delegates is based upon insufficient and highly dubious evidence; moreover, their own class interests were much more decisive than could possibly be the immediate and personal enrichment that might accrue to a Franklin or a Washington because he did or did not own a certain bond or a certain amount of previously issued currency.

Furthermore, the Constitution was not an economic document; it was a constitution. It was a political document reflecting a generally progressive bourgeois order (in which, however, existed chattel slavery); therefore, of course, a considerable part of it dealt with certain economic aspects of that order. That it was drawn up by propertied men reflects the fact that it was a bourgeois order; it was in fact drawn up only by white men, overwhelmingly Anglo-Saxon, which reflected the chauvinist and male supremacist nature of the bourgeois order. But very much the same origins characterized the men who had signed the Declaration of Independence and who sat in the Congress of the Confederation—in fact, of the total of fifty-five delegates at the Convention, thirty-nine had been members of that Congress, and eight had signed the Declaration of Independence.

But the class composition of the Convention does not make that gathering reactionary, given its time and place. And the economic content of the Constitution does not make it counter-revolutionary, for the economics of the Constitution is a continuation of the economics of the Revolution. The propertied classes were then the leaders of the nation and they were still capable of leading a struggle for national independence and for national unification.

Of course the Constitution appealed to slaveowners, merchants, bankers, creditors, budding manufacturers, and their professional servitors, since these together ruled and without their approval the Constitution would neither have been drafted nor approved. But, in the first place, the appeal was by no means unanimous amongst them, or equally great among them. And, in the second place, it must be repeated, these groups and classes are of the eighteenth century in the newly-emancipated colonies, not in the twentieth century in an advanced imperialist country.

In the *Communist Manifesto*, where Marx and Engels describe the revolutionizing features of capitalism relative to feudalism, occurs a paragraph with precise application to the question at hand. They wrote:

> The bourgeoisie keeps more and more doing away with the scattered state of the population, of the means of production, and of property. It has agglomerated population, centralized means of production, and has concentrated property in a few hands. The necessary consequence of this was political centralization. Independent, or but loosely connected provinces, with separate interests, laws, governments and systems of taxation, became lumped together into one nation, with one government, one code of laws, one national class interest, one frontier and one customs tariff.

As we have seen in considering the history of the Confederation, this paragraph relates closely to many of the forces making for greater uniformity, security and centralization. It may be compared with Washington's letter to the Congress transmitting the Constitution, wherein he said that "the greatest interest of every true American" lay in "the consolidation of our Union"; he praised the Constitution because it furthered that interest and because it "fully and effectually vested in the general government the power of making war, peace and treaties . . . [and] that of levying money and regulating commerce."

The Constitution's economic provisions—authorizing the federal government to coin money and forbidding the States to do so; forbidding the States to issue paper money, and to interfere with legal tender or contractual obligations; its tariff, treaty, police and military power; its development of the economic and political unity of the nation—served among other things to create a unified and expandable national market upon which the bourgeoisie might feed and in turn develop. All this, basic to the Constitution, is not sinister or vulgar or reactionary. On the contrary, it is the material fundament, in legalized form, of a developing bourgeoisie.

This criticism of the views of Beard is not at all identical with views holding that Beard erred because in fact classes did not exist in the new nation, or because everyone here was more or less well-off and among the "propertied," or because the real contest had nothing to do with economic and social realities but rather with differences among those who were "particularists" and those who were nationalists. Such views are argued by Robert E. Brown, Richard B. Morris, Arthur N. Holcombe, William C. Pool, Cecelia M. Kenyon, and others.

Professor Holcombe for example, wrote: "Communists strive to propagate the view that democratic republicanism, as developed in the United States, is merely an arrangement to maintain a dictatorship of the capitalist class . . . " His view is that the Constitution did not represent the capitalist class, but "was the supreme instance in history up to 1787 of the triumph of the average man."

Professor Holcombe here caricatured the views of Communists and exaggerated the accomplishments of 1787. Which Communist presented the democratic republicanism of the United States as "merely an arrangement to maintain a dictatorship of the capitalist class" is not indicated by our enthusiastic author; it is likely that this omission flowed from an absence of data and not from oversight. And that the results of the labors of Hamilton, Jay, Madison, Washington and Franklin did not represent triumphs for them and their class brothers but rather for something called, with notable unclarity, "the average man," would have surprised, I believe, the former as much as the latter.

The Marxist concept of the state as representing a dictatorship exercised by a dominant class, is by no means one sufficiently characterized, in Holcombe's terms, as "merely an arrangement." It carries with it all the complexity and subtlety of advanced modern political life; is careful to distinguish between different modes of basically similar class forms of rule; insists upon the possibility of multiclass activity and on the effectiveness, very often, with which such activity may be conducted. It does, however, see certain decisive features in particular states; and it does see the relationships maintained by classes as to the ownership of the means of production as decisive in determining, ultimately, the real and effective locus of political power.

In that sense, most certainly, the United States Constitution, as the culmination of a bourgeois-democratic revolution, was the creation of and the state instrument of that bourgeoisie, contaminated as it was by a significant amount of slaveholding.

Mr. Holcombe's own analysis of the members of the Constitutional Convention confirms this view, and not the one he advances. He states that of the fifty-five delegates, thirty-eight were of the "upper class" and seventeen were "apparently assignable to the middle classes." Of the thirty-eight, five left before the Convention ended; of the seventeen, eight left before the Convention ended. That is, according to Holcombe himself, of the forty-two delegates present until the end of the Convention, fully thirty-three were what he calls "upper class." Furthermore, his distinctions between upper and middle classes are very nebulous; thus, several of the upper class category were lawyers, presumably with considerable wealth. But of the seventeen "middle class" figures counted by Holcombe, fully fourteen were lawyers, of considerable success and fame, and with professional duties that made of them craftsmen for the propertied classes, on the whole. Another of those Holcombe excludes from the capitalist class (and he distinguishes between the middle class and the capitalist class) is Benjamin Franklin, but surely by the time Franklin was a delegate to the Constitutional Convention he occupied a class position at least the equal of any of the "upper class" men enumerated by Holcombe.

When, therefore, Professor Holcombe concluded that, "The Federal Constitution was not a triumph of capitalistic interests or of oligarchic principles . . . " it is not possible fully to agree with him. While capitalism is anti-egalitarian, it is less oligarchic, when young, than is feudalism, but it is certainly elitist and does become more and more oligarchic. The framers of the Constitution also certainly were determined to curb what they called agrarian and leveling tendencies. And the Constitution, made by propertied elements and for propertied elements, certainly was a capitalistic document in the sense that it was a charter of government for a bourgeois-democratic republic, vitiated at its birth by the decisive influence of slaveowners—a class whose role and institution are somehow ignored by Professor Holcombe.

The most elaborate critique of Beard's work is Forrest McDonald's *We The People: The Economic Origins of the Constitution* (1958). This volume consists of a detailed examination of the theses and the data put forward by Beard; it concludes by stating that both were faulty and must be rejected. In particular, Professor McDonald thinks that Beard's insistence that property in capital, as opposed to that of property in land, favored the Constitution, engineered it and forced its adoption, will not stand an examination of the evidence. In this the author makes a convincing case, and, I think, has produced a definitive work.

There were, however, two observations in Beard's work, by no means original with him, which are cited by McDonald but then ignored. These were Beard's remarks that "The propertyless masses were . . . excluded at the outset from participation (through representatives) in the work of framing the Constitution"; and that the Constitution was based "upon the concept that the fundamental private rights of property are anterior to government and morally beyond the reach of popular majorities." It is a fact that Beard himself did no more than make these remarks in passing, and then devoted himself to ascertaining the nature of factional differences plaguing varying elements among the propertied classes. In this Beard made certain acute and valid observations and, above all, opened up a significant area for further investigation.

Professor McDonald (and others before him) made important correctives of Beard's data and threw serious doubt upon his main conclusions. But, perhaps because Professor McDonald's purpose was to devote himself to a critique of Beard on Beard's own level, his own work does not deal with the fact that the Constitution-makers assumed, with Locke, that the preservation of private property was the purpose of government, and that they were themselves personally, and represented in class and historical terms, the wealthiest segments of the United States society of that period. These constitute fundamental features of the Constitution and the process of making the Constitution, both of which are assumed by Beard rather than analyzed and considered. The same is true of the work of Professor McDonald.

While Beard made serious errors in the kinds of property he assigned to the delegates to the Convention, and other significant factual errors, McDonald's own description of those delegates clearly establishes the point that the Convention was a gathering of the significant propertied components in the young Republic, and that it was these components who drafted a fundamental code of government to protect and perpetuate their social systems.

Thus, in chapter two of McDonald's volume, one finds specific economic characterizations of fifty-three of the fifty-five delegates at the Convention. We give below, from McDonald, the essence of these characterizations, omitting the details:

    1) "amassed a fortune"; 2) "son of a prosperous proprietor"; 3) "married daughter of a wealthy New Yorker"; 4) "made a tidy fortune"; 5) "a wealthy and powerful merchant"; 6) "prosperous country lawyer"; 7) "son of a wealthy clergyman"; 8) "acquired a large estate"; 9) Mayor of New Haven; considerable proprietor, though suffering economic reverses at the moment; 10) "lawyer,

financier, son-in-law of wealthy head of New York aristocracy"; 11) "one of the patricians of the Hudson"; 12) "family was one of high station"; 13) chief justice of New Jersey; 14) "a good income"; 15) "a spectacular financial operator"; 16) "a solid legal practice . . . fairly wealthy"; 17) "real financial giant of the period"; 18) "had a lucrative practice"; 19) "member of the New York landed aristocracy"; 20) "a substantial and respected Philadelphia merchant"; 21) "large and varied (financial) interests"; 22) "economic career was a fabulous one"; 23) "accumulated an estate worth $150,000"; 24) "married the daughter of a wealthy merchant, manufacturer and dealer in public securities"; 25) "wealthy by the standard of his state at the time"; 26) "moderate income" supplemented by official jobs; 27) "income from law was modest, but he inherited 6,000 acres of the vast plantation . . . "; 28) attorney general of the state; 29) "considerable substance in real estate, silver and gold"; 30) "financially independent"; 31) "wealthy member of the old Maryland planter aristocracy"; 32) "member of the old aristocracy"; 33) "after the war his income rose as high as $12,000"; 34) "he married the daughter of a wealthy Maryland family"; 35) "a tremendous fortune in land and slaves"; 36) "a wealthy member of the Virginia aristocracy"; 37) "detached from the hard world of economic reality" (i.e. Madison); 38) "one of the wealthiest men"; 39) "inherited considerable estate", suffered reverses, but was chancellor of Virginia; 40) "member of a respectable and prosperous family"; 41) "large plantation and slave owner"; 42) "member of one of the leading families of Virginia"; 43) "as accomplished a citizen as North Carolina could have sent"; 44) "young son of a wealthy family of planters"; 45) "had a substantial tidewater plantation"; 46) "quickly accumulated a large estate"; 47) "ample means"; 48) "stood at the head of the South Carolina aristocracy"; 49) "enormous patrimony"; 50) "fortunate in his marriage to the daughter of a prominent merchant"; 51) "slaves enough for two plantations"; 52) "invested wisely"; 53) "moderately wealthy"; 54) "wife brought a sufficient dowry"; 55) "young member of the relatively new but wealthy planter aristocracy in Georgia."

A mixed bourgeoisie, with a potent slaveholding class, emerged triumphant from the Revolution. Elements among them, and among those not owning means of production, developed differing and sometimes contrasting views on forms of government most suitable for them. The resolution of these difficulties was undertaken by the economically powerful and the politically significant (as of that era); this effort culminated in the Constitutional Convention. Here compromise and adjust-

ment were necessary, but they were achieved without very much
difficulty, because basic agreement existed as to the two central
facts mentioned by Beard, and then dropped by him: exclusion
of the propertyless[1] from government and a corollary, the
preservation of private property as the basic function of government.

Was there, then, no general direction of political movement in
the United States which is reflected when one compares, let us
say, the Declaration of Independence with the Constitution?
Granted that one was a manifesto justifying revolution and the
other was an instrument for the governing of a nation and that,
therefore, the two documents are not strictly comparable. Still,
do they not symbolize some drift, some kind of general trend,
and is this not towards the Right?

The answer is an affirmative one; but that answer must fall far
short of characterizing one document as revolutionary and the
other as reactionary, let alone counterrevolutionary. Rather, one
is a bourgeois-democratic document coming at the high point of
a revolutionary struggle and representing a victory of the Left in
the revolutionary coalition. The other is the legal embodiment
and crystallization of the fundamental content of that
Revolution—national self-determination, the breaking of imperial fetters upon the development of the national bourgeoisie
and the means of production and the resources of the country,
and limited enhancement of the democratic content of life in the
new country.

The Constitution comes, of course, after the fighting, after the
highpoint of enthusiasm, after the bourgeoisie finds its nation
independent and sets out to reap, as fully as possible, the
enormous benefits of that independence. The mass, and therefore, the Left, the most democratic component of the revolutionary coalition was less needed then, in terms of winning
independence than it had been in 1776; and the sober second
thoughts and exploitative drives of the bourgeoisie and planters
were coming to the fore. Hence their ever-present fears of the
masses were intensified, (especially as those masses displayed
continued militancy), and what they wanted above everything
else was law and order, stability and calm.

The Center and especially the Right of the revolutionary coalition, men like the Morrises and Hamilton, were very much moved by these considerations and opportunities. They sought the means whereby to combine the urge for stronger unity—which, as we saw, was very much wider than their own circles—with their special preoccupation with the dangers from the masses, with what they called "the excesses of democracy."

Furthermore, there was a most serious threat to the continued existence of the new Republic, coming not from the "levellers" and Shaysites, who represented no such threat at all, but from the Tories and their agents and sympathizers; from monarchists; from real reactionaries and bona fide subversives; and from the rulers of Great Britain who actively sought to dismember that Republic whose very existence was an affront.

This danger from the extreme Right is a story which has not yet been told in full. A good beginning was made with the publication, in 1922, of the already mentioned work by Louise B. Dunbar; it is a dimension which is normally omitted from considerations of the nature of the Constitution. It is unmentioned, for example in Beard's work on the subject.

Having lived for many decades under the present Constitution, it has been natural to assume that no alternative forms were contemplated with any seriousness. This view is false. James Wilson, speaking in the Pennsylvania ratifying convention on November 24, 1787, correctly posed the alternatives as seen by contemporaries. Wilson said:

> At this period, America has it in her power to adopt either of the following modes of government: She may dissolve the individual sovereignty of the States, and become one consolidated empire; she may be divided into thirteen separate, independent and unconnected commonwealths; she may be erected into two or more confederacies; or, lastly, she may become one comprehensive Federal Republic.

In 1786, serious negotiations were being conducted by National Gorham of Massachusetts and Baron von Steuben with the brother of Frederick the Great, Prince Henry of Prussia. They had in view the accomplishment of a coup and the installation of the prince as an American monarch. Von Steuben was a leading military figure here, and Gorham, in 1786, was President of the Continental Congress.

George Bancroft in his old, but still useful *History of the Formation of the Constitution of the United States* (1882), pointed out that John Jay, later the first Chief Justice of the United States Supreme Court, asked at the time: "Shall we have a king?" Jay thought not—"while other expedients remain untried"—but the posing of the question was significant. Bancroft continued:

> It was foreseen that a failure [of the movement for the Constitution] would be followed by the establishment of three separate confederacies. The ministry of England harbored the thought of a constitutional monarchy, with a son of George III as king; and they were not without alarm lest gratitude to France should place on an American throne a prince of the house of Bourbon.

In the correspondence of such figures as Washington, Madison, Monroe, Mason, Rush, Clinton of New York, and Abraham Baldwin of Georgia, was reported, in the most circumstantial form, murmurings, plans and proposals for the destruction of the Republic, either through the establishment of several confederacies, or through a unified monarchy.

In the Constitutional Convention itself there were several expressions of opinion favoring the monarchical form of government, including such an expression from Hamilton. James McHenry, a delegate from Maryland, made a list of twenty other delegates who, he said, favored some form of monarchy. It is in this light that one is to read the statement made by Franklin in a letter to Jefferson, in April, 1787, that should the Convention fail, it "will strengthen the opinion of some political writers, that popular governments cannot long support themselves." In this light, too, is to be viewed Madison's statement, made in the Convention, and seconded by Hamilton, that the delegates "were now to decide forever the fate of Republican Government."

The Constitutional Convention found it necessary to assure the public that "we never once thought of a king." The necessity for the assurance came not only from the reality of such conspiracy but also from the fierce opposition to monarchy, or to anything smacking of real counterrevolution, among the

American populace. Madison, confiding to his diary, February 21, 1787, the desires among certain "leading men" to destroy the Republic, remarked that "the great body of the people . . . are equally indisposed either to dissolve or divide the Confederacy, or to submit to any anti-republican innovations."

It is relevant to note that Jefferson, while seeing serious imperfections in the original Constitution, declared that he was more of a Federalist than he was an anti-Federalist; a major consideration for this statement was Jefferson's desire for the preservation of republicanism, threatened by either dissolution or by monarchy. It is noteworthy that Hamilton was cool to the original Constitution from an opposite viewpoint; he held it to be a "frail" charter—though perhaps better than none, and one which might be strengthened. And, contrary to a widespread myth, Hamilton was not an influential member of the Convention. He absented himself from it for two out of its four months; and Dr. W. S. Johnson, of Connecticut, was quite accurate when he remarked in the Convention that Hamilton was "praised by all, but supported by no gentleman." Hamilton himself was being truthful, not modest, when he said on the last day of the Convention, that "no man's ideas were more remote from the plan [i.e., the Constitution] than his own were known to be."

•   •   •

There was unanimity among the members of the Convention regarding the fundamentals of the society they desired: the sacredness of private property; the sanctity of contract; the inevitability of rich and poor; and their existence as reflecting immutable qualities of human society, especially of a "free" human society. Economic differences were confined to conflicts arising from different kinds of propertied interests, such as land, slaves, ships, banks, etc. The delegates agreed that the most consequential difference was that between North and South, that is, between economies based largely upon slave labor and largely upon free labor.

At the same time, the Constitution shows considerable concern for questions of political freedom, and for the problem of avoiding despotism. This concern, as has been stated, derived out of the progressive capacities of the bourgeoisie, at the time, and in particular their awareness that the populace as a whole was hostile to any curtailment of liberties. The records of the Convention are filled with evidence of the delegates' consideration of this mass attitude; with explicit recognition of the fact that unless this or that popular provision was included or this and that anti-democratic provision omitted or modified, the people—that "iron flail" as Milton called them—would simply not tolerate the result.[2]

Concretely, in terms of the provisions of the original Constitution, how were these positive influences manifested?

The document is a remarkably secular one, quite devoid of any invocation of the name of the deity. It is, also, one in which religious qualifications are conspicuously absent, either in connection with the electorate or with the elected. In the latter case, this absence of any religious requirement is made fully explicit, in the closing words of Article VI: " . . . no religious Test shall ever be required as a Qualification to any Office or public Trust under the United States."

There was a considerable broadmindedness in the United States at that time on matters of religion; so much that when Charles Pinckney offered the provision above quoted, Roger Sherman of Connecticut, "thought it unnecessary, the prevailing liberality being a sufficient guarantee against such tests." Happily, however, the majority at the Convention thought otherwise, and when one remembers the religious qualifications that then existed in the State Constitutions, it is clear that the majority was correct. Thus, while the delegates were deliberating, New York law denied citizenship to Catholics, Pennsylvania allowed only Christians to vote or hold office, Delaware allowed only Christians to hold office, in North Carolina and New Jersey only Protestants could hold public office, and in Georgia only Protestants could sit in the State Legislature.

Jews were few in the United States at this time, but there were communities of some significance in Savannah, Richmond, Charleston, Philadelphia, New York and Newport, Rhode Island. Leaders of the Philadelphia Jewish community, with Rabbi Gershom Mendes Seixas at their head, petitioned the Pennsylvania government in December, 1783, to eliminate the requirement in its constitution that those in the general assembly must acknowledge belief in both the Old and the New Testaments, thus barring Jews from membership. This gained the support of two local newspapers but it was not adopted.

While the Constitutional Convention was meeting in Philadelphia, a leader of the city's Jewish population, Jonas Phillips, presented a petition on September 7, 1787, urging that the document to come from the Convention be devoid of all religious distinctions or discriminations.

It is relevant to add that Washington during his first term, in correspondence with Jewish leaders and congregations in several cities, responded with great courtesy to their well wishes and added his own hope that the Republic would be marked not simply by "toleration" in matters of religion, but rather by real freedom. In his responses Washington did not fail to attack the vulgarity and cruelty of anti-Semitism. The latter was by no means absent in the infant Republic and it was used by the Right in the 1790s for the purpose of identifying the newly-founded Democratic Clubs with "Jewish" conspiracy—altogether in the manner of a Hitler or Coughlin.

The Constitution, then, was in its secular character more advanced than almost all the States; as for Europe, it need but be borne in mind that Catholics were barred from the English House of Commons until 1829, Jews until 1858, and nonbelievers for still another generation.

Related to this was the extreme simplicity of the oath required of the newly-elected President just prior to his assuming office, as spelled out in the first section of Article II: "I do solemnly swear (or affirm) that I will faithfully execute the Office of President of the United States, and will to the best of my Ability, preserve, protect and defend the Constitution of the United States." This may be contrasted, as the late Zechariah Chafee, suggested, with the test oath then required of all officeholders according to the constitution of Delaware: "I do profess faith in God the Father, and in Jesus Christ His only Son, and in the Holy Ghost, one God, blessed for evermore; and I do acknowledge the Holy Scriptures of the Old and New Testament to be given by divine inspiration."

The anti-aristocratic and anti-monarchical content of the Revolution is written into the Constitution. Towards the close of Article I, appears the provision: "No Title of Nobility shall be granted by the United States"; furthermore, persons holding federal office are forbidden to accept any title, office, or present of any kind from any foreign state or potentate without the express consent of Congress.[3] Additionally, in Article IV, the United States government guarantees to each of the States a republican form of government. This had considerable significance at a time when, as we have seen, the danger of monarchical restoration and the influence of monarchical ideology were strong. It carries with it, somewhat paradoxically, a restriction on popular sovereignty, in the name of popular sovereignty; that is, republicans are fully sovereign politically, but they may not abdicate that sovereignty; and if any one of the States should be threatened for any reason, internal or external, with such abdication it becomes the solemn duty of the United States government to intervene and prevent it.

Certain highly important freedoms, characteristically of an individual nature and conceiving of freedom in the sense of the absence of restraint, were written into the original Constitution. One carried with it the freedom of movement, without penalty to civil or political rights and privileges, so very important to the highly mobile American people, thus in Article IV: "The Citizens of each State shall be entitled to all Privileges and Immunities of Citizens in the several States." Further restriction upon any invidious legislation that might be enacted by a particular State against the citizens of another appears in the provision (within section 7 of Article I) permitting Congress alone "to regulate Commerce . . . among the several States."

Absolute freedom of debate in Congress is provided for (in section 6 of Article I) wherein Congressional immunity is specified—"for any Speech or Debate in either House, they [the members] shall not be questioned in any other Place." The Constitution limits the power of the legislature in two important respects: "No Bill of Attainder or ex post facto Law shall be passed." (section 9, Article II.) Behind this enactment was a long and bloody history of tyrannical usurpation. The first provision forbade the legislature from grasping the function of a Court, and finding, by fiat, a particular person or group of persons guilty of offensive behavior and therefore subject to a specified penalty.[4] The second forbade the punishment of acts declared illegal after their commission, although here, as in the case of attainder, the Congress in its handling of "dangerous thinkers" and so-called subversives has overstepped at times the borders of the prohibition.

Two additional passages in the Constitution touch on aspects of the problem of attainder. One confirms Congress' right to "declare the punishment for Treason," but it forbids such punishment to touch anyone but the individual adjudged guilty; that is "no Attainder of Treason shall work Corruption of Blood, or Forfeiture except during the Life of the Person attainted." In other words, a traitor's legal punishment was his own, and was not subject to being continued by visitations upon his descendants.

The other appears in the provisions concerning impeachment. Impeachment proceedings are to be conducted with all the safeguards of a court, with the Senate charged with the responsibility of trying all impeachments (to be presided over by the Chief Justice of the Supreme Court, if the defendant is the President). But this impeachment proceeding, while conducted like a court of law, was not to have the power of punishment, even if it found the defendant guilty, except that it might remove the guilty one from office and bar him from holding any office of honor, trust or profit under the United States. The person so convicted might then still be subject to trial by a court of law; and if convicted therein might be visited with customary penalties, such as execution, imprisonment or fine. Once more, this provision took care to separate the powers of the legislature from that of the judiciary. It showed also the intention of curbing the power of the Executive. Its passage reflected the experience acquired after several generations of impeachment proceedings in England had resulted in the execution, jailing or exiling of officeholders; it represented an effort to devise a method whereby an offensive public official might be simply removed from office, rather than exterminated or exiled.

As has already been pointed out, the crime of treason was related to the problem of attainder. One of the outstanding features of the Constitution was the care and precision with which it defined the crime of treason. The Constitution's words are (section 3, Article III):

> Treason against the United States, shall consist only in levying War against them, or in adhering to the Enemies, giving them Aid and Comfort. No person shall be convicted of Treason unless on the Testimony of the Witnesses to the same overt Act, or on Confession in open Court.

This strict definition represented a notable advance over other instruments of government then in existence. Strong opposition to it was voiced in the Convention by such influential delegates as Gouverneur Morris of New York and John Rutledge of South Carolina, and they sought alterations which would broaden its definition and make conviction easier. But they failed, and the definition remains very precise and highly limited, while the necessity for conviction reinforces the concept of treason as consisting of specific kinds of acts, rather than words or thoughts or imputed desires. The last five words in the Constitution's provisions concerning treason—"to the same overt act"—were added at the particular urging of the eldest delegate, Benjamin Franklin. Franklin made the reasoning quite explicit; according to Madison's notes of the delegates' remarks, Franklin: "Wished this amendment to take place. Prosecutions for treason were generally virulent; and perjury too easily made use of against innocence."[5]

"The most valuable human right in the Constitution," wrote Professor Chafee, "is the writ of habeas corpus, which is protected against suspension except in very limited situations." The words of the Constitution are: "The Privilege of the Writ of Habeas Corpus shall not be suspended, unless when in Cases of Rebellion or Invasion the public safety may require it." The privilege allows a prisoner, or one acting for him, to appear before a judge and secure a writ, which when served on the jailer requires that official to produce the prisoner without delay before the Court. The Court then decides, on the basis of evidence presented to it, whether or not the prisoner should be held, released on bail, or forthwith freed. The writ has functioned as a basic protector of individual rights in the United States, and has been rarely defied when once issued. The significant exceptions, however, must be noted. The writ is as good as its implementation; that is, there must be someone who seeks its issuance, and there must be someone who issues it. In cases involving especially oppressed peoples, notably Black people, and in cases involving radicals, the implementation of this has left much to be desired. Furthermore, the writ has the effect of releasing a prisoner only if he is held unlawfully. Hence, it is important to note that the habeas corpus writ itself does not safeguard personal liberty in the face of the enactment of laws providing for imprisonment or detention which are themselves violations of such liberty.[6]

Two additional significant provisions relevant to the enhancement of liberties and revolving around matters of law are in the original Constitution. One provides that trial by jury in all criminal cases (except impeachment) shall be the rule, and that such trial be held in the State where the alleged offense was committed. The other sought to safeguard the independence of the judiciary by providing that federal judges on all levels serve during good behavior and that they be compensated, at stated intervals, by a sum that shall not be diminished during their continuance in office. This lifetime tenure of appointed judges was meant to remove the officials not only from tyrannical and corrupt pressures, but also from democratic selection, influence or control; yet in terms of the century which saw the enactment of the Constitution, the weight of this kind of provision was more on the side of liberty than tyranny.

The desire to subordinate the military to the civilian, intensified by the experiences preceding the Revolution, was present among the Constitution-makers and reflects itself in that document. It appears in various provisions within section 7 of Article I, enumerating the power of Congress. Included in these powers is the control over the Army, Navy and militia, with the explicit requirement that appropriations of money for the use of the Army shall in no case be for a longer period than two years. It appears, too, in the fact that an elected President is made

Commander-in-Chief of the armed forces of the nation; and in the provision that Congress, alone, was to have the power "to declare war."

Considerable concern was expressed, especially in the State conventions considering whether or not to ratify the Constitution, over what some held to be the excessive powers of the President, with his command of the armed forces and his control over the apparatus of execution of the laws and his key role in foreign policy. Objection was raised also because no limitation was placed in the Constitution as to how often he might be elected and re-elected. Especially prophetic, in view of the experiences during the Nixon presidency, was the fear that George Clinton expressed in his essay signed "Cato" (number 4, November 8, 1787) that the President's power to grant pardons, even for treason, might perhaps be used sometime "to screen from punishment those whom he had secretly instigated to commit the crime."

Concern also was expressed by some opponents of the Constitution that the veto power of the President was dangerous. Those responsible for including this provision in the Constitution insisted that the Executive department required some protection from legislative usurpation. Certainly, contemporary argument, as shown in the 73rd essay of *The Federalist*, written by Hamilton, and as affirmed by Madison in the Convention debates, viewed the veto power as a severely limited one that ought rarely be used by the President.[7]

Despite urgent arguments in its favor, by several delegates, the Constitution set up no property qualification for any of the officeholders, whether elected or appointed, quite unlike contemporary requirements in England and in most of the States. It provides salaries for all officials; this reflected a rejection of the then-common practice of making their services voluntary, and thus possible only for the rich. Moreover, except in the case of the President who had to be native-born, no disability or invidious distinction of any kind was indicated as between native and naturalized citizens, although again heated demands were made in favor of such exclusionistic proposals.

Although proposals were made by some of the delegates that

the electorate be delimited by property qualifications, this, too, was rejected by the majority; thus, it was provided that the members of the House of Representatives were to be elected by the direct vote of the people in each of the States, and that they have the qualifications required in the different States "for electors of the most numerous Branches of the State Legislature," which, by this time, was either a quite modest property requirement or none at all so far as white men were concerned.

Confining to the House the power to introduce legislation "for raising Revenue" also was conceived of as a move strengthening the democratic content of the document, as was the provision that the House be elected every two years.

There were also proposals that other officeholders be subject to the direct vote of the people. Thus, for example, both James Wilson of Pennsylvania and Gouverneur Morris of New York—neither one ordinarily included among the pro-democratic delegates—argued for the direct and popular election of the President. This was rejected in favor of the very cumbersome and indirect electoral college device, and among those arguing in opposition was George Mason of Virginia, definitely of the "Left," and who refused to sign the Constitution. Significant in this matter, as in so many others, was the differing position on the question of the strength of the central government compared with the States.

The contradiction is in part resolved when it is borne in mind that much of the Left felt secure in its control of certain States at least, and felt also that confining the effective political unit to a relatively small size would enhance the possibilities of democratic control, while extending it to larger and larger areas necessarily would have the opposite effect.

It is a central attribute of the genius of the Father of the Constitution, James Madison, that—no doubt stimulated by his study of Hume—he intended to transform the apparent weakness of the United States from the viewpoint of a stable republican government into a strength. Madison insisted that the enormous size of the new Republic would help guarantee its durability, for this size meant great varient of sections and interests, and therefore the extreme difficulty of successful combination by any one section or interest to the point of perverting or destroying republican institutions and converting the democratic Republic into an oligarchic (or plebeian) tyranny, or into a monarchy.

The extensiveness of size, the federal structure with its numerous sovereignties, the separation of powers in the central government, and the mixed character of the locus of political power (the judiciary appointed for life, the House popularly elected every two years, the Senate selected by State Legislatures, lasting six years but each third being subject to election every two years, and the still different mode of selecting the President) would serve as an effective screening device against the precipitancy and levelism of the masses,[8] and as an obstacle for the aristocratic, monarchical or dictatorial pretensions. The bourgeoisie—historically, the "middle" class—displayed its concern about its two traditional opponents, the aristocracy and the masses, from its earliest days.

While, at the time of the Convention, an immediate problem of considerable urgency was that of preventing the destruction of the Republic by counterrevolutionary forces, it is also true that the deeper problem for the bourgeoisie—that of preventing the unpropertied, on the principle of popular sovereignty, from transforming the nature of the state from an instrument for the preservation of private property into a weapon for the confiscation of such property—was very much in their minds. This classical problem was brought freshly to their attention by mass unrest, climaxed in the Shays uprising in Massachusetts.

It is within this context that Madison's remarks made in the Convention, June 26, 1787, are to be understood:

> In framing a system which we wish to last for ages, we should not lose sight of the changes which ages will produce. An increase of population will of necessity increase the proportion of those who will labor under all the hardships of life, and secretly sigh for a more equal distribution of its blessings. These may in time outnumber those who are placed above the feelings of indigence. According to the equal laws of suffrage, the power will slide into the hands of the former. No agrarian attempts have yet been made

in this country, but symptoms of a leveling spirit, as we have understood, have sufficiently appeared in certain quarters to give notice of the future danger.

The tendency toward diffuseness of power—present even in the architects of the Constitution who sought, basically, to strengthen the Articles of Confederation—reflects also the classical bourgeois theory of freedom as an absence of restraint. Simultaneously it reflects that class' view, in its early days, that the best government is that which governs least, in contrast with the interventionist and regulatory features of government under feudalism. Present in this outlook is the concept of freedom, in its governmental sense, as something to be confined to politics in the narrowest meaning. If to these considerations is added the axiom that government exists to preserve private property, and that, therefore, only the propertied should participate in government, one completes the basic framework within which the architects of the Constitution were operating. At the same time, they were not architects in the abstract and they were keenly aware that their building would be subject to the critical inspection of all those to inhabit it, and that many of these had different class positions and needs and aspirations than did the Founding Fathers.

The principle of separation of power, while important in diffusing mass will and also in preventing personal tryanny, was viewed by contemporaries as necessary if government was to be one of law, rather than of men. This turns out to be more nearly government by lawyers, than by law, and the realities of class division do assert themselves ultimately no matter what the political structure may be. Nevertheless, the theory of government by stated law was of great consequence in the creation of the Constitution, and in the bolstering of bourgeois democracy.

This idea is stated fully and clearly in an article of the Massachusetts Bill of Rights (1780):

> In the government of this Commonwealth, the legislative department shall never exercise the executive and judicial powers or either of them; the executive shall never exercise the legislative and judicial powers, or either of them; the judicial shall never exercise

the legislative and executive powers, or either of them; to the end
that this shall be a government of laws and not of men.

To return to additional forward-looking features of the
Constitution:

Provision was made for the admission of new States, with
these newcomers to have the same rights and status as the
original States. This, also, met strong opposition, especially from
eastern delegates, but the majority was following the enlightened precedent set by the Confederation in these matters.

The specific provision looking towards the amending of the
Constitution reflects a democratic innovation. True, the method
provided is exceedingly cumbersome and this was deliberately
chosen because of the ambivalent feeling of the bourgeoisie even
at its best toward democracy; nevertheless, provision for amending the fundamental code of government reflects adherence to
the principle of popular sovereignty. It shows concern for the
principle especially attached to the name of Jefferson, that only
the living should bind the living. It is this provision which moved
Washington to write his nephew in November, 1787: "I do not
think that we [the delegates at the Convention] are more
inspired, have more wisdom, or possess more virtue, than those
who will come after us. The power under the Constitution will
always be in the people."

The whole republican framework of the Constitution, its use
of the word, "republican" (which does not appear in the
Declaration of Independence, the Articles of Confederation,
nor the earlier State Constitutions) was a blow to the friends of
absolutism. Unlike those who see in the idea of a republic
something contrasting with or opposed to democracy[9] it was
conceived of in the Constitution as the device necessary in a
large and populous country where what Madison called "pure
democracy" (i.e., direct, personal participation by every citizen)
was impossible, in order to make possible and effective the
majority's will.[10]

This not only included the sovereignty of the people, but it
also included the idea that necessarily flows from that
sovereignty—that is, the right to alter, abolish or revolutionize

any particular forms, provisions or structures of government.

This right of alteration, extending to the point of revolutionizing, was, in fact, appealed to by Hamilton in justification of the illegal steps taken by the Constitutional Convention itself, especially in exceeding its authority simply to amend the old Articles. The right of revolution is insisted upon in the writings of Madison and Jefferson and was stated at this time with particular clarity by James Wilson, a member of the Convention, and later an Associate Justice of the Supreme Court of the United States:

> A revolution principle certainly is, and certainly should be taught as a principle of the United States, and of every State in the Union. This revolution principle that the sovereign power residing in the people, they may change their constitution or government whenever they please, is not a principle of discord, rancor or war; it is a principle of melioration, contentment, and peace.

Contrary views have been expressed, but not by the makers of the Constitution; and for them and their contemporaries, who had made a successful revolution, this principle was as dear as it was near. It has had uncomfortable connotations, of course, for conservatives and dedicated supporters of the status quo. Nicholas Murray Butler, for example, the former president of Columbia University, said, in 1927, that, "Undoubtedly the weakest link in the chain of the Constitution is Article V, which provides for the method of amendment." He went on to say that "the provisions of that article as understood by the Constitution makers were entirely becoming and quite adequate." But he thought they had been interpreted by Congress and Supreme Court badly, which made them "an element of weakness and even of danger."

Mr. Butler asserted that the Founding Fathers provided a method of amendment only in order to improve on the Constitution *as it was*, to modify it in some particulars found to be faulty, but not as a means of seriously altering it. Unfortunately, Mr. Butler did not feel it necessary to cite chapter and verse for this view; what evidence there is of a contemporaneous nature is against his position. The provision for amending the Constitution was included as an expression of the popular sovereignty principle basic to the republican form of government; it was expressive, as James Wilson said, of the revolution principle lying at the base of the popular sovereignty idea.

A variant on the Butler view was expressed by George Bancroft, no mean authority on the nature of the Constitution. Bancroft wrote:

> To perfect the system and forever prevent revolution, power is reserved to the people by amendments of their constitution to remove every imperfection which time may lay here, and adapt it to unforeseen contingencies.

Further, he declared that while for Europe the necessity of revolution, and the justification for revolution remained, this was not true in the United States, where "the gates of revolution are shut and barred and bolted down" for there exists "a legal and peaceful way to introduce every amelioration."

But the revolution principle basic to the United States Constitution and its government is not confined to mere "imperfection," nor is it confined to "amelioration." The amendment power certainly does include such changes—that is, alterations in the direction of amelioration or eliminating imperfections. But the principle of popular sovereignty and the institutionalizing of that principle in the amendment power carries no limit within itself; hence, the amendment may be as fundamental and as revolutionary as the sovereign people may think necessary. Given the provision of the amendment process it should be possible for the people to achieve such changes peacefully—certainly, they can do it legally—and this is the point of James Wilson's insistence that the principle of revolution is one that tends toward peace, rather than war. The identification of violence with revolution is the work of Bancroft; it is not of the essence of revolution, which has reference to the intensity and the substantive nature of the changes in social and political structure that are made.

Mr. Bancroft also assumed that popular sovereignty had been fully achieved, once and for all, in the Constitution. While the concept of popular sovereignty imbues the Constitution, it is limited in application to the realities of who the "people" were in eighteenth century political theory—that is, white men with property—and is additionally partial in that it was assumed that governmental functions would be confined to "political" matters only and would not impinge on matters of economic and social welfare in broad terms.

There is, however, nothing whatsoever in the amendment concept of the Fathers—wedded as they were to the right of revolution—which limits its implementation to the assumptions of the Framers. When those Framers and their contemporaries viewed the principle of not having the dead bind the living, they had in mind the likelihood that passing generations would produce an awareness not only of imperfections, but of serious inadequacies; not only of the mishandling of known problems, but also the appearance of new and quite unknown ones. These means to amend the Constitution are to be handled by future generations as the generation of the Revolution and the Constitution handled urgent problems before them. Happily, however, and this is one of the significant results of that Revolution and provisions of that Constitution, legality is to be on the side of those seeking such change, be it as fundamental as it may, so long as it reflects the will of the majority of the people. That is, so long as it does not violate the basic precept of the Republic, namely, popular sovereignty.

In the area of foreign affairs, the Constitution makers were most intent upon removing this from popular influence. Here the myth of the classless state, benign and impartial, possessed of a clear "national interest" untroubled by questions of property distinctions, is especially tenacious wherefore "politics stops at the waterfront."

Hence, in the field of foreign affairs, the House of Representatives plays no part, except so far as appropriations may be required to implement policy and treaty. The Senate, on the other hand, not elected by popular vote, and having a life of six years, with only one-third of it refreshed every second year, is a necessary partner with the President in the conducting of foreign policy, and all treaties require a two-thirds vote of the Senate for ratification.

Again, however, the matter is more complex than the above

considerations indicate. For the inclusion of the advise and consent of the Senate requirement tended to restrain the powers of the Presidency, and by so much to limit the possibilities of the occupant of that office using his position to make himself a dictator. On the other hand, the two-thirds vote requirement reflected the provincialism that has been so persistent and consequential a characteristic of United States foreign policy. Europe was suspect as the home of corruption, tyranny and social decay and from that point of view it was widely felt to be healthier that the young Republic keep her distance from entanglements with Europe.

In addition to the Senate, a fundamental instrumentality for moderating any possible "excesses" of democracy that somehow got beyond the federal structure with its multiple sovereignty, (the vastness of the Republic, the separation of powers, and the indirect mode of electing one of the two houses of Congress and the Executive), was the federal judiciary, and particularly the United States Supreme Court.

The central matter of controversy in this regard is suggested in the title of an article written by Charles A. Beard in 1912: "The Supreme Court—Usurper or Grantee?"[11] The charge of usurpation has three ingredients: 1) that the framers did not understand the power to declare a law unconstitutional to be part of the judicial power; 2) that no such power, at any rate, was vested in the Supreme Court; and 3) that the practice adopted by the Court of declaring laws null and void on the grounds of unconstitutionality after they had been duly enacted by the Legislature was clearly a violation of the powers granted to the Court by the Constitution.

Nowhere in the Constitution are there any words authorizing the Supreme Court to declare duly enacted laws to be void because, in the Court's opinion, they were unconstitutional. On the other hand, it is not true that this power was not known to the framers of the Constitution; it was known to them. Furthermore, it is not true that the question was not discussed in the Convention, or in the State ratifying Conventions; it was discussed on these occasions and, with rare exceptions, the existence of the right of judicial review was assumed.

.

It is clear, as Edward S. Corwin, in particular, has demonstrated, that Beard exaggerated the number of Framers who expressed themselves as favoring the judicial right of review of constitutionality; he also exaggerated the clarity with which they were alleged to have expressed this view. But what this critique does is not destroy Beard's view; it tones it down, and makes more explicable the persistence of the doubt concerning this matter—quite apart from the obvious motives that have existed among varied groups at different times to resuscitate the doubts.

The question was raised in fairly explicit terms in the Convention, notably by John F. Mercer of Maryland, who expressed himself as opposed to the doctrine of judicial review with the power of declaring a law void. John Dickinson, of Pennsylvania, replying to him, agreed that laws should be made carefully and well so that this power of the courts would not need to exist; but, he added, laws were not always so drawn and he therefore knew no other expedient in such a case than the exercise by the highest court of its right to be the ultimate guardian of the Constitution's meaning.

Clarity of conception on this matter was expressed by Oliver Ellsworth of Connecticut, speaking in his State's ratifying convention. Ellsworth there stated:

> This Constitution defines the extent of the powers of the general government. If the general legislature should at any time overlap their limits, the judicial department is a constitutional check. If the United States go beyond their powers, if they make a law which the Constitution does not authorize, it is void and the judicial power, the national judges, who, to secure their impartiality, are to be made independent, will declare it to be void. On the other hand, if the states go beyond their limits, if they make a law which is a usurpation upon the general government, the law is void; and upright independent judges will declare it to be so.

A fair and probably definitive summarization of the facts concerning this question was offered some years ago by Benjamin F. Wright:

> It is clear that the Federal Constitution includes no clause expressly conferring this power upon the courts. There is, nevertheless, evidence adequately demonstrating that a number of the

framers assumed that the power of review would be exercised by federal, as well as state courts, and over congressional as well as state legislation. The number is not large and many of the statements are of an equivocal character. But the very fact that such views were expressed, and only very rarely questioned . . . is indicative of the existence of a belief that no express constitutional sanction would be needed for the exercise of that power.

Fundamentally, the Court was conceived of as another refiner of the people's proclivity towards "excesses" in democracy; it was another of the checks and balances, which from one point of view served as so many obstacles between the mass of the population and the locus of political power. Also present however, from the beginning, was the concern of men like Madison and Jefferson for the protection of radical minorities so that here, too, appeared the twofold purpose of the Constitution of preserving the essence of the Revolution's achievements and simultaneously bulwarking the rule of the propertied—of the "rich, well-born and able."

The multiplicity of interests was seen by Madison, as we have noted, as a source of stability for the Republic; but this did not mean that either in Madison's eyes, or in fact, such multiplicity did not create serious problems and that their reconciliation or compromise did not require much ingenuity. Among such diversities were those between large and small states, and here occurred the well-known compromise of basing membership in one house of Congress upon population and in the other giving each State the same number of members.

Aside from that dividing the propertied from the propertyless where compromise was not needed, for only the former was represented at the Convention, the keenest difference was that between the northern and the southern sections of the federation, and this pivoted around the institution of slavery. Thus, in the earliest moments of the federal history of the United States did this question of questions arise to haunt the negotiations and bedevil settlements. Madison stated at the time that the basic conflict confronting the delegates arose "principally from the effects of their having or not having slaves."

As in an earlier volume, we had noted that the same pen

which had produced the Declaration of Independence had penned advertisements for fugitive slaves, so it is a fact that while the Father of the Constitution waited in Philadelphia early in 1787 for the delegates to the Convention to gather, he was sorely troubled by problems arising from a runaway slave. And when, in 1788, Madison was resting from his labors at the Convention, we find him beset by the mistress of the French Minister to the United States, because the Madame had, as she explained to Madison, purchased "a Negro girl and only wants a boy in order that they may breed." Hence, on August 18, 1788, the Father of the Constitution wrote to his father: "Tell my brother Ambrose if you please that he must draw on Mr. Shepherd for the price of the Negro boy for the French Marchioness."[12]

Charles Thomson, secretary of the Congress, earlier had written to Jefferson of the decisive nature of the slave question for the very existence of the Republic. On November 2, 1785, the Philadelphian addressed the Virginian in these words:

> This [slavery] is a cancer that we must get rid of. It is a blot in our character that must be wiped out. If it cannot be done by religion, reason and philosophy, confident I am that it will one day be by blood. I confess I am more afraid of this than of the Algerian piracies or the jealousy entertained of us by European powers of which we hear so much of late.

Thomson felt there was reason to believe "that philosophy is gaining ground of selfishness in this respect," and it is true, as we noted in an earlier volume in examining the impact of the Revolution,[13] that certain advances were made in certain areas and for limited periods of time on this question. But these were destined to fall far short of the need, in face of the fact that already so much of the economy, social fabric and political structure of the South was shaped by the "peculiar institution." Thomson concluded his remarks with these words:

> If this can be rooted out, and our land filled with freemen, union preserved and the spirit of liberty maintained and cherished I think in 25 or 30 years we shall have nothing to fear from the rest of the world.

In the Convention, the debates concerning slavery and the slave trade were prolonged and bitter. Involved were many questions: first, that of the institution itself; second, that of the morality of the slave trade; third, that of the impact of importing slaves upon the political strength of the South, especially since the slave population was to count, in a way to be worked out by the delegates, in apportioning the number of members of the House; fourth, northern members insisted on joining to questions about slavery the question of granting Congress the exclusive right to enact navigation laws. Compromises all along the line were the result. The slave trade was permitted—as demanded by Georgia and South Carolina, and favored by some northern slave-trading states. But it was to be banned in twenty years as a concession to those delegates, especially from the middle states, who excoriated slavery, and those delegates from states, especially Virginia, who would benefit from a ban of the trade insofar as that tended to raise the price of slaves on hand. It would also help to concentrate the slave raising and trading business in their own borders. Congress alone was to have the power to tax imports, but exports were not to be taxed; slaves were to be counted in determining representation, but not equally with free people—rather five slaves would equal three free persons for this purpose.

In the course of the debates provoked by slavery, ideas were expressed which themselves continued to have considerable weight upon the development of American history. Gouverneur Morris, the very conservative New Yorker, for example, denounced the institution in language not to be exceeded in the years to come even by William Lloyd Garrison. It was, he held, "a nefarious institution," veritably "the curse of Heaven on the states where it prevailed." Morris then proceeded to compare the well-being of the slave and free regions, with an early use of an argument that was to recur for seventy years:

> Compare the free regions of the middle states, where a rich and noble cultivation marks the prosperity and happiness of the people, with the misery and poverty which overspread the barren wastes of Virginia, Maryland and the other states having slaves. Travel through the whole continent, and you behold the prospect

continually varying with the appearance and disappearance of slavery.

Ironically, the altogether aristocratic delegate, in the heat of the debate, felt that "domestic slavery is the most prominent feature in the aristocratic countenance of the proposed Constitution. The vassalage of the poor has ever been the favorite offspring of aristocracy."

George Mason, of Virginia, in the course of denouncing the slave trade, delivered a classical assault upon the slave system itself, an assault that was to be quoted innumerable times in the years to come:

> Slavery discourages arts and manufactures. The poor despise labor when performed by slaves. They prevent the immigration of whites, who really enrich and strengthen a country. They produce the most pernicious effect on manners. Every master of slaves is born a petty tyrant. They bring the judgment of Heaven on a country. By an inevitable chain of causes and effects, Providence punishes national sins by national calamities.

Madison added his view that it "would be wrong to admit, in the Constitution, the idea that there could be property in man," and the wording of the document was stretched in such a way that while it provided for the return of fugitive slaves, and for the slave to count as three-fifths a free person in apportionment, and for the slave trade to be forbidden by Act of Congress but no earlier than twenty years after the Constitution came into force—while all this was done, it was done without the appearance of the words slave or slavery.[14]

James Madison, in urging the ratification of the Constitution, wrote (in Number 42 of *The Federalist*):

> It ought to be considered as a great point gained in favor of humanity, that a period of twenty years may terminate forever within these states a traffic which has so long and so loudly upbraided the barbarism of modern policy. Happy would it be for the unfortunate African if an equal prospect lay before him of being redeemed from the oppression of their European brethren!

Happier yet, for both Black and white, if the axe had been laid, then at the beginnings of the American Republic, to the roots of the institution of slavery. Lust for profit basically explains the failure so to act; this lust in the case of slavery, as in so many additional circumstances, was to cause unutterable suffering, and the flowing of rivers of blood.

The basic limitation of the Constitution was organic to its being a bourgeois document; that is, it labored to safeguard an exploitative socioeconomic order. It was the contradiction between the interests of the owners of the means of production and of the laboring masses that was the central difficulty, though it was rarely mentioned, explicitly, at the Convention.

Madison, however, several times touched upon it, both in speeches and in letters, when he posed the problem that faced the exploiters in a republican society where the will of the majority is supposed to be sovereign. As we have indicated, it was, in considerable part, in order to get around this problem— or, at least, to delay its becoming acute—that many of the diffusing and delimiting and most involved sections of the Constitution were written.

The Fathers wanted politics to be confined to struggles among varied *propertied* groups, not between the propertied and the propertyless; they created a Constitution mirroring this hope, obscuring fundamental class antagonisms and giving the appearance of a balanced wheel—impartial, accurate and just. The grants and provisions of a democratic nature, while reflecting struggle, were also to serve as important mediums for further struggle; at the same time, they generally served to deflect the target of the struggle into channels picked by political representatives of the propertied groups.

Some among the Fathers sensed that full democracy required a substantial identity of interests; required an end to classes. They knew that with that would come practical unanimity. True, they saw existing classes as a reflection of differing natural abilities, rather than as attributes of oppressive social conditions. Hence, they saw, within the limits of freedom defined as purely political, and politics as centering on the need to preserve private property, nothing more desirable, nothing less tyrannical than the kind of bourgeois-democratic republic they were building. Hence, too, the basic task of a Constitution-maker would have to be to protect the inequality seen as an attribute of liberty, while maintaining the republican form. But the logical extension of that form would seem to be the transformation, through the mechanics of popular sovereignty, of the nature of the state from an instrument for the protection of private property into an instrument for the elimination of private property. To prevent, or to delay this as long as possible, nothing would be more effective than a bourgeois-democratic republic.

The imposition then of full disabilities upon the thirty-five percent of the population who were Indians, indentured servants and slaves, and the denial of all political rights to the fifty percent of the population who were women, were assumed by most of the Founding Fathers as more or less natural.

But none of this contradicts the essentially progressive nature of the Constitution of the United States *in its time*; acknowledging the severe limitations of this progressive quality, it is for those who follow the Fathers to improve upon their work, as their own needs and understanding suggest improvements and changes.

Washington wrote truly to the Marquis de Chastellux in the spring of 1788:

> It is a flattering and consolatory reflection, that our rising Republics have the good wishes of all the philosophers, patriots, and virtuous men in all nations: and that they look upon them as a kind of asylum for mankind.

Chapter VII

Ratifying the Constitution

THE QUESTION of the ratification of the Constitution has been treated most commonly in one of two ways, corresponding to the contrasting ways in which the document itself has been viewed. Those who have considered the Constitution holy, and the Founding Fathers saintlike, have fostered the idea that ratification of the document coming from their inspired pens was a matter of very nearly enthusiastic mass unanimity. On the other hand, those who have seen the Constitution as the result of Machiavellian maneuverings by democracy-despising, counterrevolutionary knaves, have presented ratification as the culminating act in this dismal drama, achieved despite the overwhelming opposition of the people as a whole, by means altogether deceptive and disreputable.

Since the Constitution was, in fact, neither holy nor devilish, its ratification does not present either of the two clear-cut alternatives posed above. A document that secured the favor—albeit not unconditional endorsement—from such dissimilar Americans as Thomas Jefferson and Alexander Hamilton, was not likely to have met with unanimous popular disapproval; on the other hand, a document whose ratification was opposed by such equally dissimilar Americans as George Clinton of New York and George Mason of Virginia, was not likely to have gained overwhelming popular enthusiasm.

As to the actual state of public opinion in the United States relative to the ratification of the Constitution, the historian has the greatest difficulty in arriving at conclusions with a sense of real confidence. To measure public opinion on any particular question at any particular time is exceedingly complex; to try to read back some two centuries into the varied opinions of a public split within thirteen sovereignties, each itself split into numerous economic and geographic stratifications, is something to be undertaken with the greatest diffidence; and its results are to be presented with the warning that they are little more than educated guesses.

As one would expect in dealing with a highly controversial question, contemporary opinions differed sharply as to the degree of popular support for or against the Constitution. Thus, Alexander Hamilton, confining himself to the state of New York, wrote Madison in a letter in June, 1788, that "the anti-federal party have a majority of . . . about four-sevenths in the community." Hamilton, writing thus in a private letter, and estimating the strength of opponents, would appear not to be likely to exaggerate that strength; he was one professionally and keenly concerned about the state of public opinion in New York on that particular question.

The distinguished Pennsylvanian, Dr. Benjamin Rush, on the other hand, assessing the state of public opinion in the young Republic as a whole—also in a private letter—came to a different conclusion. Writing to a friend in England, John C. Lettsom, on September 28, 1787, Rush declared: "Our new federal government is very acceptable to a great majority of our citizens and will certainly be adopted immediately by *nine* and in the course of a year or 18 months by *all* the States."

One's confidence in Rush's estimate of public opinion is somewhat shaken by the error in his prophecy concerning ratification. Actually, nine States did not ratify immediately—it was not until more than seven months had passed from the time the first State ratified until the ninth State ratified; and the thirteenth State did not ratify within twelve or eighteen months—rather it was over thirty-four months from the date that Delaware first ratified to the date that Rhode Island finally did so.

It is probably not possible to improve on the quite tentative conclusion that the very careful Richard Hildreth expressed, in the fourth volume of his *History of the United States* (written about 1850): " . . . it was exceedingly doubtful whether, upon a fair canvas, a majority of the people, even in the ratifying States, were in favor of the new Constitution."

The "canvas" that was taken, in the 1780s, was not fair, in terms of a historian of the mid-nineteenth century; for one writing in the late twentieth century it was far from an adequate test of public opinion. Of the approximately three and a half million people in the United States at the time the Constitution was being voted upon (the first United States census, taken in 1790, showed 3,929,000 population), when one eliminates the women and children, the enslaved and indentured men, the Indians and free Black people—all of whom were not allowed to vote; and adds to this the numbers forbidden to vote because they were unable to pass certain suffrage requirements (especially those involving property possession, which in some areas, Maryland, for example, disfranchised many), one finds that there was a total potential electorate of perhaps half a million.

Of this potential electorate, in all contests a large percentage did not actually vote, for reasons that varied from apathy or illness to distance from the polling places.

In the elections of delegates to the state ratifying conventions, those for ratification were at an advantage because the form of apportionment in all of the States, except Delaware, was such as to favor eastern and urban areas. The extent of mal-apportionment was great, as Charles W. Roll, Jr. demonstrated; the most notable was in Georgia and South Carolina where about 13 percent of the States' inhabitants were able to control the make-up of the conventions.

In the elections of delegates to the ratifying conventions dealing with the Constitution, it was estimated by Charles A. Beard that perhaps 160,000 votes were cast. Beard, who did not tend to emphasize the popular nature of the Constitution, believed that about 100,000 cast ballots for delegates known to be favorable to ratification. Forrest McDonald, in his recent very critical reexamination of Beard's work, comments on this aspect of it as follows:

After a survey based on tabulations from all discoverable voting records preserved in the archives of the thirteen states and of all votes recorded in extant newspapers of the period, it is my conclusion that Beard's estimate of the total vote was remarkably accurate.

• • •

The Congress existing under the Articles of Confederation received the suggested Constitution on September 20, 1787. Some delegates attempted to censure the Convention for having exceeded its authority—limited to amending the Articles—by having submitted an entirely new constitution, but this was defeated and on September 28 the proposed Constitution was forwarded to the legislatures of each State for submission to special ratifying conventions.

The struggle over the ratification of the Constitution within the State legislatures was long and bitter. Part of the opposition to adoption stemmed from sources reflecting opposition to the creation of a viable republic truly capable of existing in independence of Great Britain. Another part was of the opinion that uniting so enormous an area was simply impossible and that all efforts to do so were doomed to failure and hence had better not be made in the first place. These groups engendered ideas of the creation of two or three or even more separate confederacies, perhaps joined by some kind of league but in reality quite distinct and sovereign.

Elements within ruling circles in Britain, Spain and France were quite cool to the establishment of a strong United States which, with inevitable growth, would challenge their positions both in the Western Hemisphere and in worldwide diplomacy and trade.

Mainly, however, opposition to the Constitution was indigenous coming particularly from those who were suspicious of all increments of governmental power, especially when such power was not local, and who were distraught because the suggested Constitution contained no Bill of Rights, such as existed in the Constitutions of most of the States. There were also some among the white people who found incongruous the fact that the proposed document, while never mentioning slavery, contained several provisions which in fact admitted its existence and even tended to strengthen it. These included proposals calling upon the Federal government to assist in suppressing insurrections, in returning fugitives to their owners, not to prohibit the international slave trade for at least twenty years after adoption and the provision enhancing the representation of slave-owning societies by counting every five slaves as three "persons" when fixing members of the House.

One of the delegates at the ratifying Convention of New Hampshire, Joshua Atherton, stated that he could not vote to ratify a document that entered into a covenant with, as he put it, "manstealers." On the other hand, the clause in the Constitution stating that Congress should pass no laws prohibiting the slave trade prior to 1807 was objectionable to some delegates in southern conventions because it seemed to imply—as it was meant to, in fact—that Congress would prohibit such trade after the two decades had passed. Thus, Rawlins Lowndes, of South Carolina, opposed ratification and one of his grounds was that northerners wanted to end the slave trade since they had no slaves themselves and "therefore want to exclude us from this great advantage." Mr. Lowndes went on to defend the trade in principle, something even slaveowners rarely did in public until another fifty years had passed, declaring that "For his part he thought this trade could be justified on the principles of religion, humanity and justice . . . ."

Of the original thirteen States, only four did not contain in their Constitutions a specific Bill of Rights; of these four, two were major slaveholders—Georgia and South Carolina (the remaining two were New York and New Jersey). In South Carolina, the defense of this omission included all the usual arguments, such as an insistence that the government was given only specific enumerated powers and that seeking to make explicit certain rights might imply or suggest hostility to rights not enumerated. But there the defense of the omission of a Bill of Rights included an additional argument which illustrates—as the history of the United States does in general—the organic connection between the enslavement of Black people and the curtailment of the rights of all other people. Speaking at the ratifying convention of South Carolina, General Charles C.

Pinckney said that a reason for omitting a Bill of Rights which "weighed particularly with the members from this state" was the fact that such bills "generally begin with declaring that all men by nature are born free. Now," the General went on, "we should make that declaration with a very bad grace, when a large part of our property consists in men who are actually born slaves." General Pinckney might have observed that the birth certificate of the nation begins with the affirmation that all men are created equal; as a matter of historical fact that feature of the Declaration became increasingly obnoxious to the slaveholders as their precious institution matured and they finally opted for an attempted counterrevolution in the 1860s.

Three States ratified the Constitution unanimously: Delaware (the first to act) did so on December 7, 1787; New Jersey did the same eleven days later and Georgia also unanimously approved (January 2, 1788). Five of the thirteen original States which ratified the Constitution did so together with urgent suggestions that it be amended at the earliest opportunities along the lines of a Bill of Rights; this was true in Massachusetts, which finally ratified on February 7, 1788 (by a vote of 187–168) but which did so only after nine recommended amendments were appended, including that which became the Tenth Amendment: "The powers not delegated to the United States by the Constitution, nor prohibited by it to the States, are reserved to the States respectively, or to the people."

New Hampshire ratified on June 21, 1788 and since she was the ninth State to do so, her action in a formal sense satisfied the requirements for ratification as established by the Philadelphia convention; in ratifying, this State also urged the passage of a Bill of Rights. Virginia acted in a substantially similar way when it ratified, finally, on June 25, 1788 (89–79).

After news that the ninth State had ratified and that Virginia also had done so, it was possible to squeeze out a pro-ratification vote in New York, on July 26, 1788 by 30 to 27. Even under those conditions, that close vote came only after New York City threatened to secede from the State and join the Union on its own—the first time, but not the last that the city made a threat of secession. Furthermore, New York in ratifying, urged that a Bill of Rights be added.

North Carolina, whose convention met in July, 1788, refused to ratify; it announced that it would ratify only when persuaded that there would be a Bill of Rights added to the document. When in the first Congress of the United States such a bill was submitted—on September 25, 1789—North Carolina called a second convention and at this time (November 21, 1789) ratification was carried by a vote of 194 to 77.

Rhode Island was the one State which had not had a delegation at the Philadelphia convention drafting the proposed Constitution. Its government, firmly in the hands of smaller farmers and bitterly opposed to the eastern commercial and professional groups, resisted all efforts by the latter to call a ratifying convention. Instead its legislature provided that a popular referendum was to be held in which voters would directly state whether or not they approved the Constitution. This was held on March 24, 1788 but it was boycotted by all Federalist elements. While there were some 6,000 eligible voters in the State, about 2,900 actually seem to have cast ballots and of these less than 250 were in favor of ratification. It was not until the first Congress had been in session almost one year and a Bill of Rights had been passed by that Congress and was being considered by the States that Rhode Island agreed to the holding of a convention for purposes of discussing ratification. At the end of May, 1790 Rhode Island finally ratified—nudged on further by pending legislation in the Federal Congress which would have severed Rhode Island from all trade connections with the United States government. Even under these conditions, the vote in favor of ratification was 34 to 32 opposed.

With personalities as diverse as Jefferson and Hamilton favoring the Constitution—the former especially if it had a Bill of Rights and the latter opposing such addition—and with the addition of the Bill of Rights promised and with the further understanding that Washington would serve as the first President, the Constitution's ratification may properly be regarded as the consolidation of the Revolution.

Chapter VIII

The New Government: Organization and Early Activities

FOLLOWING THE ratification of the Constitution by the ninth State, New Hampshire, on June 21 and by Virginia four days later, the Congress under the Articles announced the Constitution as ratified on July 2, 1788, in the following words:

> Whereas the Convention assembled in Philadelphia pursuant to the resolution of Congress of the 21st of February, 1787, did on the 17th of September in the same year report to the United States in Congress assembled a constitution for the United States. Whereupon Congress on the 18th of the same September did resolve unanimously, "That the said report with the resolutions and letter accompanying the same be transmitted to the several legislatures in order to be submitted to a convention of delegates chosen in each state by the people thereof in conformity to the resolves of the convention made and provided in that case." And whereas the constitution so reported by the Convention and by Congress transmitted to the several legislatures had been ratified in the manner therein declared to be sufficient for the establishment of the same and such ratification duly authenticated have been received by Congress and are filed in the Office of the Secretary; therefore, Resolved that the first Wednesday in January next be

the day for appointing electors in the several states, which before the said day shall have ratified the said constitution; that the first Wednesday in February next be the day for the electors to assemble in their respective states and vote for the president; and that the first Wednesday in March next be the time and the present seat of Congress the place for commencing proceedings under the said constitution.

In accordance with this announcement, on February 4, 1789, presidential electors, having been chosen in each of the ratifying States, cast ballots for the office of President, with the understanding then, that the individual with the second highest vote would be declared Vice President. On April 6, 1789, the votes were counted in the Senate and it was found that George Washington had been elected unanimously and that the person with the next highest votes (34) was John Adams, who was then declared to be Vice President.

While, according to the announcement of Congress, the new Congress was to have met on March 4, as of that date there was no quorum, since most members were still en route to the then capital, New York City. During the week of April 1–8 a quorum appeared and the first Congress met, with 30 out of 59 members of the House and 9 out of 22 members of the Senate, on hand.

On April 30, 1789, Washington was sworn in as the first President, taking his oath on the balcony of the Federal Hall in Wall Street, New York City. He delivered his inaugural address within the Senate chamber; it contained less than 1,500 words. He pledged his best endeavors to faithfully serve the Republic, "since the preservation of the sacred fire of liberty and the destiny of the republican model of government are justly considered, perhaps, as *deeply*, as *finally*, staked on the experiment intrusted to the hands of the American people." The single substantive proposal, or suggestion, in the brief address came in the next paragraph where Washington urged that due consideration be given to the widespread desire for amendments to the Constitution. "It will remain with your judgment," Washington told Congress, "to decide how far an exercise of the occasional power delegated by the fifth article of the Constitution (for amendments) is rendered expedient at the present juncture by the nature of objections which have been urged against the system, or by the degree of inquietude which has given birth to them."

Washington turned to organizing his departments and from July through September, 1789, he created the Department for Foreign Affairs (later State), the War Department, that of Treasury[1] and a Post Master General—raised to department status in 1795. Jefferson was selected for the first department (John Jay served as Acting Secretary, pending Jefferson's return from his Ministerial post in Paris), and Henry Knox, Alexander Hamilton and Samuel Osgood for the others.

The slavery question haunted the Congress from its very first session when Madison vainly tried to obtain passage of a bill requiring a duty of ten dollars upon every imported slave. Madison urged that the increase of the slave population intensified the Union's instability and the danger of slave rebellion but in the face of those who were profiting from the trade and those who were seeking additional forced labor, Madison's efforts failed.

In the March, 1790 session of the First Congress, a Quaker-inspired petition praying for the prohibition of the slave trade was warmly debated in the House. It finally appointed a committee to inquire into whether or not such action by Congress would be in accord with the Constitution. The committee decided that Congress had no right to prohibit the slave trade prior to 1808, that it was forbidden to interfere in the treatment of or to emancipate slaves, but that it might restrain U.S. citizens from carrying on the African slave trade for the purpose of supplying foreigners. Further, stated the committee, Congress had the power to legislate in favor of humane treatment of the "cargo" during its passage into States permitting the trade and also had the power to forbid foreigners from fitting out vessels in the United States for transporting persons in Africa to any foreign port. Congress accepted this report as conveying its sense of the question and ordered the petition thereupon tabled. In this debate, Representative Aedanus Burke of Georgia said he resented any discussion whatsoever of slavery, insisting that this "would sound an alarm and blow the trumpet of sedition through the Southern States."

The first significant piece of legislation passed by the new Congress was its original tariff measure, which placed a duty of from five to fifteen percent on imported commodities, and gave a ten percent reduction on goods imported in ships built and owned in the United States; this act, reflecting a kind of economic unity and independence, was passed by Congress on July 4. Early in September, Congress began its debate upon a projected Bill of Rights; ten were adopted on September 25, 1789 and proposed to the States for their consideration. This process was completed on December 15, 1791 when, a sufficient number of States having ratified the first ten Amendments, they were declared adopted and became part of the Constitution on December 15, 1791.

Coincident with this federal and national activity in political terms, the Protestant Episcopal Church was organized, in Philadelphia, in 1789, being the independent American expression of what had been the colonial arm of the Anglican Church. In December, 1790, John Carroll of Maryland was consecrated as the first American Roman Catholic Bishop, after an exchange of letters between him and Church officials reflecting the determination of the United States affiliate to be loyal in terms of religion, but independent in terms of any secular or political relationships. This was done, it should be added, at a time when Catholic churches existed only in Pennsylvania and only four States had full religious tolerance.

At about the same time another and not altogether unrelated display of independence appeared with the creation, in protest against jim-crow Christianity, of both the African Methodist Episcopal Church under Richard Allen and the A.M.E. Zion Church under Absalom Jones in the late 1780s and the 1790s.

On a cultural and scientific level one also found evidences of a sense of freshness; thus, in the early 1790s appeared a proliferation of scientific organizations, as the formation of the Massachusetts Historical Society (1791), the Chemical Society of Philadelphia (1792) and the Academy of Medicine also in Philadelphia in 1792. Notable advances were made in this same decade in such disciplines as geography and botany, and the beginnings of a demand for an *American* art and theatre and literature—indeed, even language—date from the years just after the Paris peace treaty.

Note has been taken earlier that the thirteenth State joined the Union when Rhode Island took this action late in May, 1790. The Atlantic States were completed—with the exception, of course, of Florida, not to be purchased from Spain until 1819—when Vermont was admitted as the fourteenth State on March 4, 1791. The Green Mountain State—beset on all sides with land claims by Massachusetts, New Hampshire and New York—had declared itself an independent republic in 1777, but with the settlement of these disputes and claims and the effective establishment of a Union, she was admitted.

As emphasized, without the understanding that the first Congress would add a Bill of Rights to the Constitution it would not have been ratified. And, as also noted earlier, the wisdom of fulfilling this understanding formed the main substance of Washington's inaugural address. The work was guided in the first Congress by Madison who used the provisions of several State Constitutions as well as the specific suggestions made by States when ratifying. The result was that the Congress submitted to the approval of the State legislatures twelve amendments, of which the first two were not ratified by a sufficient number of States. Those sought to establish precise regulations for future Congresses in terms of population enumeration for the number of Representatives, and to lay down binding rules as to when salaries of members of both Houses might be altered.

The Ten Amendments reflected lessons gained through the struggles against monarchical tyranny in Britain and in the colonies during the struggle for independence. They embodied, also, much of the political thinking of the Encyclopedists of France and the Enlightenment figures of the European continent, upon whom Jefferson had drawn when drafting the Declaration of Independence. The provisions of these Amendments are so familiar and their text so readily available that no extensive commentary would appear to be needed.

One point of detail, not frequently observed, may be underlined. This refers to the last phrase in the Fifth Amendment: " . . . nor shall private property be taken for public use, without just compensation." Under this provision, it was possible and constitutional for the United States government, in the Thirteenth Amendment, to abolish slavery and in doing so to confiscate property in slaves without compensation. This was made explicit in the fourth section of the Fourteenth Amendment where it was stated that neither the United States nor any single State was to be held liable "for the loss or emancipation of any slave" and that all claims based on this (some of which were then in federal courts) "shall be held illegal and void." The slaves certainly were private property, but their emancipation—i.e., their confiscation as property—was not done "for public use." There does not seem to have been debate on this point in the Fifth Amendment but it shows again the decisive difference between property in things and property in persons.

The debate in the Congress concerning what became the first Ten Amendments was prolonged, but not especially heated. Very nearly all members of the House and Senate agreed with Washington's reminder in his inaugural address that the Constitution's ratification would not have been achieved without the promise of such changes.

A few in the House, like the conservative Roger Sherman of Connecticut and Fisher Ames of Massachusetts, did oppose amendments, insisting that they were unnecessary and unwise, but their arguments were without influence. Madison proposed at first that the substance of the amendments be incorporated into the text of the Constitution itself, but this was found to be too clumsy and the expedient of making the proposals actual amendments was accepted.

Certain suggestions were considered which were more advanced and positive than those finally adopted. A few Representatives suggested that the people should be guaranteed the right not only of assembly and petition but also of instructing their Congressmen on public matters. This was rejected on the grounds that it would vitiate the representative and deliberative quality of the House and would subject its members to direct popular control—held to be dangerous. In the Senate, certain provisions that had passed the House were killed; these included a provision that would have exempted conscientious objectors from compulsory military service, another that would have explicitly forbidden any of the three departments from using powers vested in the other two, and a third which would have forbidden any *State* to "infringe the right of trial by jury in criminal cases, nor the rights of conscience, nor the freedom of speech or of the press." A proposal that would have limited the powers of the Federal government only to those "expressly" given in the Constitution was rejected, Madison and others insisting that in any effective government "powers must necessarily be admitted by implication"; this heralded the "states' rights" argument that was to appear and reappear throughout U.S. history.

Taken as a whole, the Bill of Rights actually constitutes not rights in terms of what may be done; it constitutes more accurately a Bill of Wrongs—forbidden to the Federal government. That is, in keeping with bourgeois theories of freedom, the Bill of Rights affirms what may not be done; it treats freedom as an absence of restraint, not as the capacity to act. This concern with restraint, however, was limited to white men with property. People of color, women and the needy and indigent, of course, had to be restrained and were meant to have none of the powers affirmed in the Constitution; they were objects of history, not subjects of history.

• • •

While the Constitution provided for a Supreme Court and a judiciary, their establishment required an act of Congress; this, too, was done by the first session of the first Congress with the passage late in September, 1789 of the Federal Judiciary Act. This provided for a Supreme Court to consist of a Chief Justice and five associates and the establishment of thirteen district and three circuit courts. It also established the office of Attorney General. John Jay was appointed Chief Justice that same month and Edmund Randolph of Virginia became the nation's first Attorney General.

The executive and judiciary departments having been organized, the postal service established, the amendments added, the first tariff legislation passed, those who governed were faced with the task of enhancing the fiscal credit of the new nation so that it might function within a capitalist world. In accomplishing the latter, another objective was to manage it in a way that the merchant and financial communities within the nation would find their interests tied to the durability of the Union. Hence, in January, 1790, Alexander Hamilton, as Secretary of the Treasury, submitted the first portion of his fiscal program.

Hamilton's first report on the public credit, submitted to Congress on January 14, 1790, was devoted to the problem of the debt the new government inherited from that of the Confederation. This had three components: 1) the foreign debt—owed mostly to Dutch, Spanish, and French bankers—came to almost $12,000,000; 2) the domestic debt of the federal government, amounting to almost $44,500,000; and 3) state debts, amounting to about $25,000,000.

Hamilton proposed that those holding notes and currency showing indebtedness by the Federal government (both foreigners and citizens of the United States) were to be allowed to exchange their depreciated paper for new government bonds, paying interest, with the exchange to be made at the *face* value of the depreciated paper. As to the state debts still outstanding, Hamilton's plan called for their assumption by the Federal government. There was no significant opposition to issuing new bonds to foreigners at face value of their original investments, both because such investments had been indispensable to the successful waging of the war and because unless this were done the credit of the new Republic in European money markets would be seriously impaired.

But the idea of exchanging depreciated paper held by U.S. citizens at face value raised much opposition because speculators had been busily buying up such paper from veterans, farmers and poorer folk generally. These speculators had been especially active in the months prior to the submission of Hamilton's plea because they had prior knowledge that this would be the nature of the government's program. Hence, many among the population in general who had sold this paper at a fraction of its face value, now found that the United States government was proposing to exchange that paper—much of it in the hands of the speculators—for new United States interest-bearing bonds at the full face value whereby rich people would make an enormous profit. Madison proposed to the House that the legislation carry a clause discriminating between original owners of the papers and later purchasers, but the House rejected this by a large majority.

The scheme for the assumption of state debts also aroused significant opposition, much of it of a sectional character. The southern states had already settled their debts but the northern and especially the New England states had not. If assumption were adopted, therefore, New England—meaning especially the merchants and speculators of New England—would make another killing, and this at the expense of southerners and westerners in particular whose taxes would have to pay off the enhanced national debt. This meant, also, increasing federal power at the expense of the States, and especially states other than those in New England. For Hamilton on the other hand, it meant just what he wanted: strengthening the central government, enhancing its credit status in the money markets, tying the merchant, shipping and manufacturing interests more strongly to the Federal government and also enriching the people in whose circles Hamilton moved and whom he always strove to serve.

That phase of Hamilton's program was defeated in the House, early in April, Madison himself breaking with the Washington administration on this question; the vote was very close — 31–29. The Washington-Hamilton contingent then sought a compromise with the Jefferson–Madison group. Of great interest at that moment was the locale of the capital city for the new nation. The Constitution provided (Article I, Section 8) that Congress was "to exercise exclusive legislation in all cases whatsoever, over such District (not exceeding ten miles square) as may, by cession of particular States, and the acceptance of Congress, become the Seat of the Government of the United States . . . ." Maryland, in an act passed in December, 1788, and Virginia, in an act passed one year later, authorized the cession of necessary territory for the federal capital. Congress in July, 1790, authorized the President to direct the surveying of an area "not exceeding 10 miles square" on the Potomac and this work was begun under the leadership of Pierre Charles L'Enfant, one of the French volunteers in the Revolution, and later continued under Andrew Ellicott and the Black mathematician and surveyor, Benjamin Banneker.

Two weeks after Congress had adopted the seating of the Federal capital in the South—in an area provided by both Maryland and Virginia—the House reversed itself on the assumption proposal and voted for it, 34–28; it became law with Washington's signature early in August, 1790.

A consequence of the adoption of Hamilton's funding and assumption proposals was the rise in the national debt to over eighty million dollars. To serve that debt consumed nearly eighty percent of the annual expenditure of the government. Indeed, during the final decade of the eighteenth century, to pay the interest alone on the national debt took over forty percent of the total national revenue. All this was as Hamilton wished for it helped focus political and economic power within the Federal government.

Despite the compromise, the passing of the Hamiltonian assumption scheme produced bitter denunciations from many among the planters—and the closeness of the passage of the measure shows the intensity of this antagonism. The Virginia legislature adopted a resolution, in December, 1790, asserting that the Hamiltonian plan favored moneyed against agrarian interests, threatened the perpetuity of republican institutions and was accomplished though there was no provision in the Constitution for the assumption of state debts.

In 1791, Hamilton introduced logical extensions of his fiscal program, including a proposal for a national bank and heavy excise taxes by the Federal government. These provoked even more opposition than the first part of his over-all economic plan for the new government; indeed, one result was insurrection. But the analysis of this falls within the province of the ensuing volume in this series. Here note should be taken that the projection of Hamilton's proposals stimulated the polarization of politics in the United States, so that distinct parties on a national scale made their hesitant and secretive beginnings, basing themselves upon party and factional splits which had already emerged within statewide and regional areas.

Jefferson remained in Washington's Cabinet until the close of 1793, but by 1791 his disagreements with Hamilton over financial and economic policy and over international relations had become fundamental. The ensuing months witnessed the exacerbation of these differences, with Jefferson expressing very strong opposition to Hamilton's plans for a Bank of the United States and his pro-British policy. In Jefferson's opinion these threatened the republican character and the independent sovereignty of the nation; Washington finally deciding otherwise, Jefferson felt it necessary to remove himself from that administration. Fuller exposition of the roots of these differences and treatment of the ensuing political divisions in the nation will form significant themes in a subsequent volume.

The Hamiltonian-inspired political activity reflected as it bulwarked significant economic trends in the new nation. Largely at State initiative and expense, important improvements were made in transportation facilities, so that between 1785 and 1786, for example, Virginia built a turnpike connecting Alexandria with the Shenandoah Valley and Maryland authorized such work to connect Baltimore with the west. Canals and bridges were built in many different areas and the first experiments were made in the 1780s with steam navigation, particularly by James Rumsey and John Fitch.

Notable advances were made in the late 1780s and in the 1790s in shipbuilding, rum distilling, paper, and textile industries as well as in the manufacture of boots and shoes. By 1790, the three States of Pennsylvania, New Jersey and Delaware had a significant iron industry, turning out over 350,000 tons of plate iron and nails in that one year. Heavy metal products, as forges and anchors, also were successfully manufactured within the States, since the transit costs for these items were so great that competition from the more highly developed British industry could be overcome.

The export of flour showed the transition from subsistence to commercial farming; such exports from the main port of

Philadelphia more than doubled between 1786 and 1789. Though cotton production in real quantity awaited the development of a successful cotton gin, to come later in the 1790s, even in this commodity, a steep increase appeared, so that while only five bales were exported in 1785, over three hundred bales were exported three years later.

The Asian trade became fairly important and before the end of the 1780s a United States Consul was operating in Canton.

Banks made their appearance in this same decade—the Bank of North America in Philadelphia in 1780, the Bank of New York (with Hamilton as a director) in 1784 and that same year the Massachusetts Bank in Boston. Companies engaged in the insurance business proliferated; between 1781 and 1790 twenty-five such companies were organized in New York City and Philadelphia.

Industry still was in its infancy in the United States and there existed a severe shortage of advanced machinery and skilled mechanics—and English legislation made their exportation or emigration serious crimes. Still, by 1789 Samuel Slater—a British expert in textile manufacturing—had secretly made his way to the United States and within another two decades, the United States had reached a powerful adolescent stage so far as industry was concerned—though an adolescence much inhibited by the presence of slavery in one-third of the nation.

Chapter IX

The New Government and the American Indian Peoples

 F ROM THE original invasion of the Western Hemisphere by the European powers in the fifteenth century until the last decade of the nineteenth century, so far as the government of the United States is concerned, the relationship with the indigenous peoples—the so-called American Indians—was a matter of pre-eminent consequence.

After the inauguration of Washington, at the end of April, 1789, until his Second Annual Address to Congress in December, 1790, there were perhaps twenty-five messages and papers from the President to Congress. Of these about half were devoted to the American Indians. His first special message, May 25, 1789, placed before Congress the texts of treaties negotiated between the War Secretary Henry Knox and "several nations of Indians." Thereafter his messages to Congress of August 7, August 10, August 20 and 21 of 1789, as well as those of September 16 and 17 dealt altogether with this same decisive matter—whether or not to negotiate treaties, the need of strengthening the armed forces of the young Republic so as to treat with the Indian peoples from strength, and the staffing of various federal delegations to deal with Indian peoples—especially in these instances, those in the South, particularly in Georgia.

President Washington's main concern in 1790 was with "pacifying" various Indian peoples, especially the Creeks in the southern regions of the Republic, and how best to manage the appropriation of their lands and the shifting of their trade away from Spanish and British merchants to those of the United States.

Also indicative of the decisive nature of the so-called Indian question, especially in these early years of the nation, is the fact that of the thirteen laws passed during the first session of Congress, four dealt with that question. A survey of the immediately preceding years must be offered so that the questions confronted by that session in 1789 may be better understood.

Some of the American Indian peoples had maintained a precarious neutrality during the Revolution, others had allied themselves with the Americans and still others—probably a majority—with the British. In all cases, of course, their actions were guided by their own estimates of where their best interests lay and, in particular, how they might preserve their lands and at least relative independence. In this case, as throughout the history of the encounter between the European and the American Indian, the latter had not achieved firm unity and that failure was fatal in general and specifically in the last quarter of the eighteenth century.

Actual hostilities between the British and the American forces terminated in February, 1783, when a preliminary discussion of questions of a peace settlement were probed. It was the British who first told representatives of Indian peoples that the fighting was over; the U.S. Congress, (under the Confederacy), did not so act until May, 1783, when it directed the War Secretary to convey this information.

It was not until almost a month after the signing of the Paris Peace Treaty, that the Congress issued a proclamation, dated September 22, 1783, affirming U.S. domination over all the territory hitherto claimed by Britain. This proclamation declared that no person might settle in or purchase lands claimed by Indian peoples without the "express authority" of the Congress. Almost three years later, on August 7, 1786, an Ordinance issued by Congress established an Indian department of the

Federal government, under the control of the War Secretary, and divided it into a northern and a southern district. Traders in these districts might not be employees of the department handling Indian affairs, had to be of good character and had to have a license. An additional section of this Ordinance stated that should any action of the Indian department seem to interfere or conflict with the powers of any State, the federal superintendent of Indian affairs was ordered to "act in conjunction" with such State.

The famous Northwest Ordinance of 1787 (adopted on July 13), concerned with the manner and form of the settlement of the area north of the Ohio River, necessarily contained provisions relevant to the status of Black and Indian peoples. It provided that the territory was initially to be ruled by a governor, secretary and three judges, appointed by Congress, and that when a total of five thousand free adult males were in the Territory it was to have a legislature consisting of two houses. It provided also that ultimately from three to five States might be formed from the Territory; a minimum of 60,000 inhabitants was needed for admission to the Union. Such new States were to be "on an equal footing with the original States in all respects" and freedom of religion, trial by jury and the support of public education were to be provided.[1] Nothing was explicitly stated as to Black people—and there was no mention of free Black people—but slavery was prohibited in the Territory.

In the section of the Ordinance treating with education, there appeared the following paragraph:

> The utmost good faith shall always be observed towards the Indians, their lands and property shall never be taken from them without their consent; and in their property, rights, and liberty, they never shall be invaded or disturbed, unless in just and lawful wars authorized by Congress; but laws founded in justice and humanity shall from time to time be made, for preventing wrongs being done to them, and for preserving peace and friendship with them.

More in accord with the realities of the past and the future of European and white American relationships with the Indian peoples, than the above paragraph of monumental historical irony is the fact that their "supervision" was put into the hands of the War Department and the first governor of the Northwest Territory was General Arthur St. Clair, a well-known "Indian fighter."

The 1787 Ordinance was itself the culmination of several years of planning and pressures from settlers in the West and from land speculators. The settlers, beginning in 1780, had furthered various secessionist threats; North Carolina faced for a time during and just after the Revolution a move by western settlers to create their own state of Franklin; a similar movement finally led to the admission of Kentucky as a State in 1792 and of Tennessee four years later. The latter results awaited the "pacification" of the Indian people of the area and this began in earnest, once the peace of 1783 was signed.

Among the immediate pressures producing the Ordinance, however, and especially the quoted paragraph concerning the promises of justice towards Indians, were the activities of the Iroquois, Huron, Wyandotte, Delaware, Shawnee, Ottawa, Chippewa and Cherokee peoples who held unity meetings in November and December, 1786. From the latter meeting emerged a joint letter to the "Brethren of the United States of America." It said:

> It is now more than three years since peace was made between the King of Great Britain and you, but we, the Indians, were disappointed, finding ourselves not included in that peace, according to our expectations.

This letter continued: "We thought we were entering upon a reconciliation and friendship with a set of people born on the same continent with ourselves, certain that the quarrel between us was not of our making." In the course of our discussions, this letter went on, "we imagined we hit upon an expedient that would promote a lasting peace between us."

The Indians making up the peoples enumerated above considered themselves a confederacy—just as others had confederated into a United States of America with an Articles of Confederation. Therefore, the "expedient" that they thought would "promote a lasting peace" was that:

All treaties carried on with the United States, on our part, should be with the general voice of the whole confederacy, and carried on in the most open manner, without any restraint on either side; and especially as land matters are often the subject of our councils with you, a matter of the greatest importance and of great concern to us, in this case we hold it indispensably necessary that any cession of our lands should be made in the most public manner, and by the united voice of the confederacy.

A note of indignation and complaint then crept in despite what seems an immense effort at self-restraint; "You have managed everything respecting us your own way. You kindled our council fires where you thought proper, without consulting us, at which you held separate treaties,[2] and have entirely neglected our plan of having a general conference with the different nations of the confederacy."

The letter concluded: "Brothers . . . let us have a treaty with you early in the Spring. Let us pursue reasonable steps; let us meet half-way, for our mutual convenience." And in particular and very specifically, "We beg that you will prevent your surveyors and other people from coming upon our side of the Ohio River."

Early in 1787 that letter from confederated Indians reached Congress, which in July passed the Ordinance for the organization of the Northwest Territories. Having appointed General St. Clair the Governor, it sent him special instructions in October, 1787, "to examine into the real temper of the Indian tribes inhabiting the northern Indian department." Congress continued that the Governor may examine the "treaties which have been made" (that is, those of 1784 and 1785, concerning which the Indian letter of December, 1786, had complained) but, Congress continued, they "must not be departed from, unless a change of boundary, beneficial to the United States[!] can be obtained."

Of fundamental importance in problems of the Northwest following the signing of the 1783 peace treaty, was the fact that Great Britain refused to yield the seven border posts stretching from Lake Champlain to the end of the Great Lakes; these were within the territory of the United States, as agreed upon in that treaty. Britain refused to give them up, however, claiming that so long as the United States did not complete the settlement of debts owing British citizens these posts would be held. The real reason for Britain's obduracy was her hope that she might yet sever the Northwest from the upstart Republic; furthermore, possession of the posts gave English merchants an advantage in terms of controlling the fur trade with the Indian peoples (worth about 200,000 pounds sterling annually). Finally, the bases gave England a bargaining point in efforts to convince Vermont—not yet in the Union—to remain independent. It was not until the conclusion of the Jay Treaty, signed in November, 1794, that Britain agreed to yield these posts, and to do that by June, 1796. The particular history of that treaty belongs in a subsequent volume.

Frontiersmen continued to pour into the new Territory and to encroach upon lands held by different Indian peoples. By the summer of 1788 organized raiding parties were actually invading Indian settlements and villages; counterattacks followed and by 1789 the United States was engaged in a serious Indian war. There were two main encounters in this war of 1789 through 1791; in both, the forces of the United States were routed. The first resulted from an expedition commanded by General Josiah Harmar who moved to the attack northward from Fort Washington—just outside the then fledgling settlement called Cincinnati—but his progress was known to Indian scouts who fell back and permitted him to march many miles and encounter no foe. At the end of October, 1790, Harmar, disappointed and low in supplies, started back south; he attempted a surprise move by several hundred of his militia men, turning sharply north, but the Indians were waiting for them and in a sharp battle the militiamen lost almost two hundred men while the Indian loss was very few.

Now it was the turn of the Governor of the Territory himself, and General St. Clair—who earlier had assured Congress that "I am persuaded their (the Indians') general confederacy is entirely broken"—set out late in the summer of 1791 with a major force of three thousand men into the Maumee country. He built three forts on the way, to guard his rear and as logistical supports, but while a day's march outside Fort Wayne he became careless, permitted his men to pitch tents and posted few guards. The Indians, though vastly outnumbered, were able to surround the U.S. forces and under the leadership of a Miami warrior, Little Turtle, attacked on the night of November 4, 1791. The defeat for St. Clair was complete; he and others managed to escape and flee to Fort Jefferson, but they left behind over 900 casualties while, again, Indian losses were negligible.

The defeat of the United States in the 1790–91 campaign in the Northwest had decisive impact upon the attitude of Great Britain. Hardening in her refusal to yield the posts which she held on U.S. territory, Britain intensified her plans to sever much of the United States from boundaries agreed upon, seeking to create either a vast Indian buffer state, or preferably, to detach the Northwest from the United States and make it a part of Canada. At the same time, the defeat convinced the United States that nothing but an all-out campaign against the Indians of the Northwest Territory would frustrate both those Indians and the plans of the British. This assault was undertaken in 1794 under the command of Major-General Anthony Wayne. After a campaign lasting one year, and after the betrayal of the Indians by the British—who feared becoming involved again in a full-scale war with the United States (and who had their hands full in a Europe being remade by the French Revolution)—Wayne inflicted devastating defeats upon the Indians, culminating in August, 1794, in the Battle of Fallen Timbers. This resulted in the formal capitulation by the Indians early in 1795 in the so-called Treaty of Greenville in which they were forced to surrender practically all of present Ohio and much of Indiana.

The second main area of conflict between the new United States government, as well as certain of its States, especially Georgia, and the Indian peoples lay in the South and Southwest. Involved here were the efforts of Spain, then possessing east and west Florida (the latter reaching from Pensacola to New Orleans) and Louisiana, to retain this territory, to dominate the trade therein with the Creek people and to use its control of the great port of New Orleans as a device to thwart the growth of the Northwest itself, as well as present-day Kentucky and Tennessee.

The northeastern States were willing to yield control of New Orleans to Spain and in 1786 in the so-called Jay-Gardoqui Agreement this concession was to be formalized by treaty. But in the Confederacy only seven northern states—who thought the proposed treaty would enhance their trading possibilities in Europe—approved the treaty proposal and since nine affirmative votes were required, it did not pass. Still, the proposal itself and the affirmative votes of the northern States angered and frightened the western settlers and land speculators as well as southern States, especially Georgia, which had conflicting land claims with Spain. The result was intrigue with Spain reaching treasonous depths and involving especially James Wilkinson—later a major-general and an ally of Aaron Burr in the latter's complex anti-Jeffersonian schemes; the result also was renewed attacks upon the Indian peoples of the South and Southwest and ruthless efforts to force them from their lands.

In part because of European developments following the French Revolution, and near war between England and Spain, the latter withdrew its support of Creek resistance to the United States just as in the North, Britain did with other Indian peoples. But the secessionist threats in the West and the fierce resistance made by the Indians led Washington—faced with the Indian war in the Northwest—to seek settlement through negotiations. He appointed some of the leaders in secessionist efforts as important officials in the Southwestern Territory of the United States (created in 1790) and even appointed Wilkinson a lieutenent-colonel in the United States Army.[3]

With Spain no longer an ally, the Indians, too, sought a negotiated settlement. Vehemently opposed to any settlement—except complete dispossession of the Indians and termination of all their rights—was Georgia whose legislature had been bought by the owners of three land speculating companies. But with the continued unity of the infant Republic at stake, Washington pressed for peace, and the Indians, without Spanish aid, and facing the fanatical hatred and considerable power of Georgia, agreed with Washington. Hence, when Washington sent a personal peace emissary South to the leader of the Creeks (Alexander McGillivray, son of a Scottish father and Indian mother, who had chosen to live with and be part of his mother's people) that leader met the emissary and agreed to return with him to New York and to meet personally with President Washington.

The emissary of the President, plus the Indian leader and some thirty other Indian leaders, traveled north in an elaborate procession and were led to Federal Hall in New York by a huge assemblage of people. Here, face to face with Washington himself, the Treaty of New York was signed, August 7, 1790. The Creek Indians ceded a considerable portion of land between the Ogeechee and Oconee rivers in eastern Georgia but they received a guarantee, "in perpetuity," to their remaining lands, specifically including the over twenty-five million acres which Georgia had "sold" to the three land speculating companies for a total payment of less than $210,000. As a mark of personal regard and esteem, Alexander McGillivray was appointed a brigadier-general in the United States Army at a salary of $1,200 a year. Moreover, this treaty provided that any citizen of the United States who settled on the lands of the Creek people without permission of the Creeks thereby forfeited the protection of the United States; and that, in any case, entry into the territory of the Creeks was to be made only with the display of a valid passport.

This treaty was signed personally by President Washington, Secretary of State Jefferson and Secretary of War Knox on the one hand and by McGillivray and twenty-three other Creek leaders on the other, with the Chief Justice of New York State and the Mayor of New York City, signing as witnesses. It brought the curses of the Georgia legislature; James Jackson, representing Georgia in Congress, could not contain his fury as he denounced Washington and his government for this affront to his State. Jackson added that the contents of the Treaty were bad enough but that it really was intolerable that President Washington had "invited a savage of the Creek Nation to the seat of government, caressed him in a most extraordinary manner, and sent him home loaded with favors."

This Treaty brought an end to Georgia-Indian warfare for the first time in a decade, but the end was quite temporary. Soon the racism, aggressiveness and rapacity characteristic of the rulers of Georgia and the South—and, for that matter, of the Federal government in general—would emerge triumphant and the genocidal policy would again be pursued.

Chapter X

The New Government and
the Afro-American People

IN "THE LAND of the free and the home of the brave" there lived at the time of the first United States Census, in 1790, almost four million people; of these about 750,000—or some 19 percent of the total—were Black people, of whom about 700,000 were slaves. The vast majority of the Black population at that time was concentrated in the South Atlantic States, from Maryland through Georgia; about 670,000 lived in this region, of whom over 640,000 were slaves. New York, New Jersey and Pennsylvania were home to some 50,000 Afro-American people; of these nearly 30 percent were free, testifying to the effect of the emancipation acts passed in those States during and just after the Revolution (though New Jersey's act did not come until 1804). In New England, something over 13,000 Black people lived; here the impact of the emancipation spirit coming out of the Revolution had nearly terminated slavery, for of the 13,000 Black people, less than 4,000 were still slaves. Only two States in the Union had no slaves at all—Vermont and Massachusetts[1]— while the largest number of slaves still working in New England labored largely on the tobacco farms of Connecticut. In that State in 1790 over 2,600 slaves were counted in the Census.

Kentucky and Tennessee were not yet states; both were rapidly filling up with European and African-derived peoples, and by 1790, Kentucky already counted 12,000 slaves and Tennessee had almost 3,500. Both areas then had a total of less than 500 free Black people.

The Black people in the United States at this time—and until well after the Civil War—were overwhelmingly a rural folk, even more so than the nation as a whole. Nevertheless, there was only one area of settlement called a city in the first Census which contained no slaves; this was Boston wherein then lived nearly 800 free Black people.

The slaves performed all kinds of labor; they were coopers and cobblers, chandlers and pilots, glaziers and tailors, blacksmiths and bricklayers, musicians and longshoremen, coal miners and lumbermen, waiters and caterers, nurses and domestic workers. Their labor was skilled and unskilled; above all, they formed some thirty-five percent of the South's total population, and since Black women and children all worked, some fifty percent of the producing masses in the South were Black slaves.

The main crops produced by slaves at this time within the limits of the United States were rice, tobacco, hemp, indigo and some cotton. Their labor and what it produced and the trade in slaves, both within the United States and from Africa, were major components of the entire economic activity of the United States.

Slavery in the United States was a system of forced labor in which the workers were the absolute property of the masters; it existed basically for the purpose of producing commodities for sale on a worldwide capitalistic market. That market then was insatiable and growing; the slaves were owned by the masters for the profit that could be derived from their labor. There were accompanying "benefits" for the masters, such as psychological stimuli and sexual advantages, but the fundamental point about slavery in the United States was that it made possible the appropriation of the surplus value produced by workers who received no wages at all and required nothing more, in law, than subsistence. According to the masters themselves this meant an expenditure of about fifteen dollars per slave, *per year* and, again according to the masters, slaves became profitable by the time they were nine years of age.

The slaves' workweek was six days long (sometimes seven as a form of punishment or during special seasons in particular areas and with particular crops) and lasted generally from "can see to can't see" or from dark to dark; this meant about fourteen to fifteen hours each day in the summer and spring and about eleven to thirteen hours each day in the winter and fall.

The system was maintained by an elaborate machinery of control which was psychological, religious, social, legal and—above all and ever-present—had behind it force and the threat of force. Racism served to divide the nonslaveholding whites from the slaves and was a basic component of the method of control. Divisions were played upon among the slaves by the masters—domestic versus field hands (which had some color discrimination usually attached to it); drivers versus rank and file; and the masters sought constantly to induce some Black people to serve as spies and informers. At times they succeeded, for all people have had their traitors and the Black people did, too; yet in the face of the provocations and temptations, however, their numbers were small. The basic result of a common oppression was to produce a magnificent sense of solidarity. The fire of enslavement did not consume the Black people; on the contrary, they endured its every indignity, insult and blow and emerged from it steeled, rather than consumed.

In the period of concern for this volume all forms of resistance created by the Afro-American people were present; individual and collective resistance of myriad forms appeared. There was flight, individual and group; there was self-injury, suicide and infanticide; there was individual resistance, often against a particularly brutal overseer or master, frequently involving use of club or axe, fire or poison. There was collective resistance in the form of maroons—outlying and belligerent fugitive slaves who resisted capture and who, often, maintained themselves by a kind of guerrilla warfare against adjacent plantations. And there was the highest form of collective resistance—conspiracy to rebel and efforts at rebellion.

In the 1780s and 1790s, especially in Georgia, the Carolinas and Virginia, maroons constituted a serious problem for the authorities. State militias waged veritable wars against camps of fugitive slaves; South Carolina in 1787 offered a reward of ten pounds sterling for each of these rebels, dead or alive.

Some slave conspiracies were reported, particularly in Virginia in the 1780s, but it is in the 1790s—with the widespread Indian wars and the impact of the French Revolution and the massive slave uprising in Haiti—that such reports become most numerous.

By the 1780s and 1790s the free Black people had organized themselves for the purpose of assisting in the freedom struggles of their enslaved brothers and sisters, to help themselves and to combat practices and laws which were discriminatory and racist. Thus, by 1787 Free African Societies existed in Philadelphia, Boston, New York and Newport, Rhode Island. In that same year a petition "of a great number of Blacks" was presented to the legislature of Massachusetts protesting the denial of equal educational opportunities for their own children. Also in 1787, free Black people consolidated their own Masonic order and soon thereafter Black men and women had founded grammar schools and Sunday schools to serve their own communities, since the States and cities refused to do this. Collective petitions against the slave-trade, the kidnapping of free Black people and against slavery itself began to assail the ears of Pharoah from every corner of the United States in the 1780s and 1790s; in some cases white people joined in these efforts.

The ideological struggle against racism was in full swing also in these early years of the Republic with white and especially Black people bringing forward every possible argument to show the absurdity of its concepts. Absalom Jones and Richard Allen were prominent in this regard; perhaps best known was the effort of Benjamin Banneker to educate Thomas Jefferson. In 1790 and 1791 Banneker tried to convince Jefferson of the error and horror of his racism. He understood Thomas Jefferson not to be "inflexible in sentiments" and so hoped that he would "embrace every opportunity to eradicate that train of absurd and false ideas and opinions which so generally prevails with respect" to Black people. Alas, while the letters Jefferson wrote at this time show that Banneker somewhat shook the author of the Declaration of Independence, he did not persuade the

Virginia slaveowner that his "way of life" was based upon utter falsehood and that persistence in it was wrong for any person and quite monstrous for the drafter of an immortal manifesto of revolution.

While the national antislavery movement properly may be said to begin in the 1820s—with the launching of *Freedom's Journal* in New York City in 1827 and the appearance of the astonishing *Appeal to the Colored Citizens of the World* by David Walker in 1829 and then the first National Convention of Colored People the next year—it also is true that antislavery sentiment was present in the area making up the United States from the beginnings of the institution. Certainly, the first Abolitionist was the slave himself and herself; and by the end of the seventeenth century there began to appear organized expressions of opposition to slavery as in the famous Germantown protest of 1688.

Thereafter, as was shown in the first two volumes of this series, expressions and organizations of an antislavery character abounded in the North and South; from white people and from Black people; and from men and women. People like Benjamin Lay, Ralph Sandiford, John Woolman, Abigail Adams, Thomas Paine, James Otis, George Mason and dozens more said everything that could be said—or ever was to be said—in denunciation of the monstrous system. In the years of the Revolution, in particular, antislavery expressions and legislation flourished.

In the post-Revolutionary generation, in addition to the pioneering actions of Black people themselves, there appeared the very influential writings and activities of the Quaker, Anthony Benezet (1731–1784), who founded an early school for the education of girls, another for the education of Black children, denounced the genocidal practices aimed at Indian peoples, denied the validity of racism and—above all—conducted a passionate campaign against slavery.

Benjamin Rush (1746–1813) of Pennsylvania, the great pioneer in medicine and mental health, and a signer of the Declaration of Independence—of whom John Adams said, upon learning of his death, "taken all together Rush has left not his equal in America, nor that I know in the world,"—like

Benezet was a universal reformer. He denounced the treatment of Indians, urged publicly-supported education, wanted prison reform, called for an end to the death penalty, insisted that there was mental as well as physical illness, sought the termination of all corporal punishment, was the father of several educational institutions of higher learning (including Dickenson and Franklin and Marshall Colleges) as well as a school for the education of women. In his *Thoughts Upon Female Education* (1786) Rush insisted that those who opposed education for women exposed "the prejudice of little minds" and that this prejudice "springs from the same spirit which opposes the general diffusion of knowledge among the citizens of our republic."

Central among the concerns of Benjamin Rush was slavery and he forthrightly urged its abolition; he also attacked concepts of racism as clearly unproven and highly dubious. In his own practice as a physician he found the work of a Black man, James Derham, of fine quality and praised his skill in published writing.

Benjamin Franklin (1706–1790) devoted much of the last decade, in particular, of his fabulous life to the cause of antislavery. He was the first president of the Pennsylvania Society for Promoting the Abolition of Slavery, incorporated by the State legislature in 1789. Three months prior to his death, in his eighty-fourth year, Franklin sent to the editor of the *Federal Gazette* in Philadelphia one of the last pieces of writing from his pen. This was a parody poking fun at the arguments of those who defended slavery; it was in the form of a defense by a member of the Algerian government of its practice of enslaving those American seamen captured by its privateers in the Mediterranean (and for whom President Washington later agreed to pay a handsome ransom price).

Earlier there had been formed, in 1785, the Rhode Island Society for Abolishing the Slave Trade; that same year there came into being the New York Society for Promoting the Manumission of Slaves. The first president of the New York organization was John Jay; the second was Alexander Hamilton. In 1788 a similar organization was created in Delaware. In 1789 in Maryland appeared a Society for Promoting the Abolition of Slavery and in 1793 such a society was formed in New Jersey. Indeed, in January, 1794, there met in Philadelphia the first national gathering devoted to attacking this cancer of slavery and racism; it was called the American Convention for Promoting the Abolition of Slavery and Improving the Condition of the African Race. Representatives were present from New York, New Jersey, Pennsylvania, Delaware, Maryland, Connecticut and Virginia.

All of these organizations and individuals, Black and white, and their collective and individual efforts, were of basic importance in achieving through legislation the abolition of slavery throughout the North, and in helping induce the manumission of thousands of slaves in the South—especially in the border areas of Maryland, Delaware, Virginia and Kentucky.

The theoretical approach of these organizations tended to be moderate but statements appeared in print in the late 1780s and early 1790s that anticipated the most militant approaches that were to become dominant in the Abolitionist movement only some fifteen years prior to the Civil War. Thus, in the widely read magazine published in Philadelphia, *The American Museum* in 1789, appeared an essay by a "Free Negro" which not only denounced slavery and denied the inferiority of Black people, but also went on to demand: "Do the rights of nature cease to be such, when a Negro is to enjoy them? Or does patriotism in the heart of the African, rankle into treason?"

As the letters of Abigail Adams show, women were writing privately in this era in an effort to educate the male population to the injustice under which women suffered. Occasionally this reached the point of publication, as the two-part article signed "Constantia," entitled "On the Equality of the Sexes" and published in the *Massachusetts Magazine*, in March and April, 1790. This essay, actually written around 1780, insisted upon the reality of its title and drew its logical conclusions—the propriety of full political, civil, and economic equality of the female half of the human race. The author noted that as between a brother and a sister: "The one is taught to aspire, the other is early confined and limited. As their years increase, the sister must be wholly domesticated, while the brother is led by the hand through all the flowery paths of science."

Publishing an essay eight years later in *The Gleaner*, a magazine issued in Boston, this "Constantia" allowed herself to be so encouraged by the appearance of some academies and schools for the education of females that she wrote, rather prematurely: "I may be accused of enthusism; but such is my confidence in THE SEX that I expect to see our young women forming a new era in female history."[2]

The post-Revolutionary era witnessed not only antiracist and antimale supremacist thinking and some action; there appeared in print, also, the suggestion that all people, including those who were poor and those who labored, and their children, had the right and the capacity for education. Timothy Dwight in Connecticut and Caleb Bingham in Massachusetts insisted that education which ignored women and girls was only half sufficient for a republic; the Reverend John Murray urged, in the 1780s, that education had to be placed within the reach of all citizens. It was Washington's aide-de-camp, Col. David Humphreys, who put these lines into a book published in 1790:

> *No feudal ties the rising genius mar,*
> *Compel to servile toil, or drag to war;*
> *But, free, each youth his fav'rite course pursues,*
> *The plough paternal, or the sylvan muse.*

Chapter XI

Social Classes and Wealth: Reality and Mythology

IN THE 1950s, the conventional wisdom among Establishment social commentators in the United States held that poverty here was nonexistent, or at most, persisted in certain "pockets" involving an insignificant fraction of the population. Left analysts insisted at the time that this was untrue but it was not until the heights of the Black liberation movement of the early sixties and the great student upheaval of the same period—and the radicalization that accompanied the growing antiwar movement—that writers within the mainstream began to discover "poverty in America" and finally even the President of the United States acknowledged its existence.

Approximately the same phenomenon has marked dominant history writing, especially, again, during the Cold War years and the neo-Conservatism that prevailed then. An aspect of the mythology spun by these historians, such as David Potter and Robert E. Brown and Daniel Boorstin, was that the United States was exceptional in the colonial and Revolutionary and post-Revolutionary generations since here upward social mobility was characteristic and poverty was either quite nonexistent (and unmentioned) or so inconsequential as to be brought forward as further proof of the "exceptional" condition prevailing here.

The fact is that social mobility never has characterized United

States history; on the contrary, the rich have been rich and have been getting richer and the poor have been numerous and their percentages do not decrease but rather tend to increase as the social order ages. Of course, in the United States, unlike Europe at the time, actual chattel slavery existed and this involved about 20 percent of the total population at the time of the Revolution; if one adds to this the indentured servants and the American Indian population, one finds that at least 35 percent of the total population were held in law and fact at subsistence or below subsistence levels.

Jackson Turner Main in his *The Social Structure of Revolutionary America* (1969) reported that in the years 1763–1771 and 1782–1788 about 10 percent of the population held between 40 and 60 percent of the wealth, varying from area to area. In a later brief essay, published in 1971, Main remarked that his data were faulty in certain significant respects; most serious was the fact that he had omitted consideration of "slaves, servants, and many other poor people"—the latter phrase not further clarified. Moreover, his original data had ignored the fact that there was "a tendency on the part of the assessors to undervalue the property of the rich"—a tendency not confined to the early period in United States history!

He concluded that perhaps another 5 percent of the wealth should be added to that held by the rich in the Revolutionary era. The fact further is that as the years passed, the degree of concentration increased everywhere—the data for Boston, for example, as James A. Henretta showed (in 1965), demonstrated that the richest 10 percent of the population there held 42 percent of the wealth in 1687 and 57 percent in 1771.

Later research on Boston in particular, as that conducted by Allan Kulikoff (1971), showed that in 1771 the top 10 percent of the taxpayers owned "nearly two-thirds of the wealth" and that the tendency towards concentration of wealth increased after the Revolution, so that "not a less stratified, but an even more unequal society developed in Boston after the Revolution." This was at a time, let it be remembered, when Boston had about 20,000 inhabitants, with about 40 percent of the population directly or indirectly connected with foreign trade and when no industrial group employed a large number of workers and when the mean number of workers in enterprises came to thirteen.

By 1790 there were two factories of some size in the city; in these by far the majority of the workers were women. Thus, the largest of them, manufacturing duck cloth, employed 17 men and over 380 women and girls. The only other large factory—a cotton and wool card factory—employed 1,000 workers, of whom some 750 were children; indeed, about one-fifth of all the children living in Boston were working in that factory.

The pattern everywhere in early United States (and in the colonial era) was the same; widespread inequality becoming more and more markedly unequal as the decades passed and as subsistence farming tended to disappear. Allan Kulikoff, in the already mentioned essay, concluded:

> Although in the seventeenth century wealth in American towns was typically less concentrated than in sixteenth-century English towns, where the poorer half of the population owned less than a tenth of the wealth and the richest tenth owned between half and seven-tenths, the English pattern soon reappeared in America and intensified.

As one may expect and as Kulikoff affirmed, "The growth of poverty was a major problem" and by around 1790 the absolutely impoverished numbered about 10 percent of the entire population. Studies concentrating upon the South—as that by Lee Soltow (1971)—show similar patterns, though in that region, with slavery, the inequality of wealth distribution was the most intense in the nation.

Throughout the eighteenth century newspapers complained frequently of the "many beggars troubling our doors," of the "increasing number of young beggars in the streets," and these same papers, speaking for their class, invariably ascribed the cause of this poverty to the character of the poor—being poor they were both without money and without merit! Thus, "blaming the victim" was normal for the ideologues of the rich in the colonial and post-Revolutionary period as it has been in the post-World War II United States.

Edward Pessen, whose work on wealth distribution in the United States has been of outstanding importance, estimates

(1973) that on the eve of the Revolution the richest 10 percent owned some 40 percent of the net wealth in the middle colonies (New York, New Jersey and Pennsylvania) and about 45 percent in New England. Other studies indicate that one must add about 10 percent to these figures for the South. Investigation shows without any doubt that the concentration of wealth continued during and after the Revolution. I would conclude, therefore, that in the nonslaveholding portion of the nation in about 1795 the richest 10 percent owned 55 to 60 percent of the net wealth and that in the South this figure should be about 70 to 75 percent.[1]

Chapter XII

Mass Activity and Struggle: Urban and Rural

COLLECTIVE ACTIVITY and struggle on the part of the legally free working people, in urban and rural areas, in the United States appear in the eighteenth century. Even in the South where the widespread existence of slavery and the especially blatant racism made this struggle most difficult, such efforts appeared just before, and in the post-Revolutionary generation.

In several southern cities in the eighteenth century, skilled white workers protested the competitive use of slaves and demanded that the practice cease, a recurrent theme in southern labor history. Laws forbidding this were passed from time to time in the South but they were poorly enforced because such use of slaves benefited their owners and those who hired them.

There is record of at least one instance of free Black workers in the South, even before the Revolution, combining to improve their conditions. This involved Black chimney sweepers in Charleston who, in 1763, "had the insolence" as the city's *Gazette* put it, "by a combination amongst themselves, to raise the usual prices, and to refuse doing their work, unless their exorbitant demands were complied with." Such activities, continued the paper, "are evils that require some attention to suppress," but just what was the outcome of this particular effort is not known.

Societies of mechanics, artisans and other workers, that played so important a part in the origins and organizational features of the Revolution itself, existed in the South as elsewhere. The immediate post-Revolutionary period was marked by the formation of numerous workingmen's benevolent societies and the beginning of their transformation into weapons for increasing wages and otherwise improving working conditions—that is, into trade unions. Again, this movement, while most widespread in the North, was by no means absent from the South. On the contrary, the 1780s and 1790s witnessed bakers, bricklayers, carpenters, and other skilled workers actively campaigning, in collective fashion, for increased pay in Virginia and the Carolinas. Such groups and efforts faced, in addition to employer resistance, legal prosecution as when, in 1783, the carpenters and bricklayers of Charleston, South Carolina, were charged with conspiracy because they had combined for the purpose of raising their wages. Bakers of the same city struck in 1786, while its Mechanics' Society demanded higher pay in 1794.

At about the same time a Society of Journeymen Tailors was formed in Baltimore, and there is record of a strike conducted by it certainly as early as 1795. The central issue was the rate of wages, and in this case an increase was won. Seamen in Baltimore also succeeded in winning a pay raise, by a strike, in 1795.

Similar activity on a wider scale occurred in northern cities during this period and many of the details are given by Philip Foner in the first volume of his *History of the Labor Movement in the United States* (1947). Involved were strikes by printers in New York City late in the 1770s and what Foner calls "the first authentic strike" occurring in 1786 among the journeymen printers in Philadelphia. Strikes by carpenters in the same city occurred in 1791 and by carpenters and masons in New York City four years later.

These temporary united efforts by workers were replaced in the 1790s by the creation of permanent organizations of workers which may be called trade unions in the modern sense. Organizations of this type, which lasted for years, included shoemakers in Philadelphia, tailors in Baltimore, printers in New York City and cabinet and chair makers in the same city; the latter organization, founded in 1796, endured over thirty years.

During the same twenty or thirty years spanning the origins of the Revolution, the fighting, and the decade that followed the peace, mechanics, artisans and other workers in the cities developed a political sense of class consciousness, as well as the sense of economic collectivity reflected in the benevolent societies and nascent trade unions. Realities in New York City have been especially studied, notably by Alfred Young and Staughton Lynd. Others have shown that in cities such as Charleston and Philadelphia, by the 1770s, working people were expressing vigorous opposition to the idea that politics belonged only to the rich and propertied. Thus, in a book published in 1901, Charles H. Lincoln, studying *The Revolutionary Movement in Pennsylvania, 1760–1776*, quoted a joint letter from Philadelphia mechanics, printed in the *Pennsylvania Gazette*, September 27, 1770 stating that:

> it has been customary for a certain company of leading men to nominate persons and *settle the ticket* for assemblymen, commissioners, assessors, etc., without even permitting the affirmative or negative voice of a mechanic to interfere, and, when they have concluded, to expect the Tradesmen to give a sanction thereto by passing the ticket; this we have tamely submitted to so long that those gentlemen make no scruples to say that the Mechanics (though by far the most numerous, especially in this county) have no right to be consulted, that is, in fact have no right to speak or think for themselves.

This kind of thinking was part of the essence of the American Revolution; following the success of that Revolution it reappeared in cities throughout the new Republic. Indeed, Young and Lynd expressed the opinion that in New York City, "the demands of the mechanics formed the stuff of politics in the last quarter of the eighteenth century."

In the 1790s the mechanics, artisans and tradesmen of New York City created collective organizations not only in order to lift their incomes but also to further their political interests. One mechanic, for example, writing in a New York newspaper early in 1785, remarked that "the pedantic lawyer, the wealthy merchant, and the lordly landholder, have already had their interests sufficiently attended to" and that therefore it was time to reflect that "the respectable mechanics", were "not only adequate, but entitled to the reins of government."

One year later another New York newspaper published a communication which stated that the people of the city did not need as their legislators "men who study Grotius, Puffendorf, Montesquieu and Blackstone" for they would "neither be able to comprehend the laws they may make, nor to practice them when they are made." On the other hand, he went on, "the laws of the mechanics, like the makers of them, will be simple and unperplexed; therefore," he concluded, "let us have mechanics, and mechanics only for our legislature."

While in the political discussion pursued by people like Washington, Madison, Hamilton and Jefferson during and after the creation of the Constitution and the struggle around its ratification, political parties were held to be natural for monarchies and unnatural and baneful for republics, one finds this kind of insightful analysis in a letter from an anonymous contributor to the *New York Journal*, September 25, 1788:

> Men, upon whom fortune has smiled, and favored with wealth, are too apt to be puffed up with vanity and pride, and ambitiously to aspire at procuring the honorable and lucrative offices of government, fancying, that wealth alone will make up for the deficiency in abilities, and that those are never bestowed on the middling or lower class of people, or such as are not blessed with wealth equal to themselves. If therefore the last two classes of people have any regard to their independence and liberty, parties must be formed, and a contention arise between the different classes.

• • •

Outside the cities, where in this period the vast majority of the population lived, contention enough existed. The postwar depression was one source of the unrest; another was the constantly increasing concentration of the ownership of wealth. A third was the system of finances and taxes that marked the Hamiltonian approach to government and characterized not only the

Federal government under Washington but several of the State governments as well.

Representative of the popular unrest is Samuel Cullick Ely, a participant in the Revolution against Britain and later a rebel in three States; representative of the class bias of historiography is the fact that Ely is yet to find a biographer.

Ely was born poor (in North Lyme, Connecticut in 1740) and died poor fifty-five years later. He was a preacher in Somers, Connecticut by 1765 but the church that had first heard him split asunder and a council of elders offered it as their opinion that Ely was not qualified, either in piety or in learning, to be a minister. He seems again to have been preaching just before the Revolutionary fighting and again to have been dismissed. Timothy Dwight—the eminently respectable and successful divine, destined to be President of Yale (1795–1817)—wrote that this Ely "declared himself, everywhere, the friend of the suffering and oppressed, and the champion of violated rights. Wherever he went," Dwight continued, "he industrially awakened the jealousy of the humble and ignorant against all men of superior reputation, as haughty, insolent, and oppressive."

In a word, Samuel Ely seems to have taken the teachings of Jesus as seriously as John Brown; no sensible Christian from the president of Yale to the Governor of Virginia can abide that.

After fighting in the Revolution, in New England, Ely appeared as a leader of discontented and indebted farmers in Massachusetts. In January, 1782, he urged the people to discard the extant constitution and make one of their own. He insisted that the salaries of officeholders were too high and that the Courts favored creditors and detested debtors. His followers grew: they met in conventions, as in Hadley, Massachusetts in February, 1782, and pronounced Ely's ideas plain and sensible. By February 14, 1782, Ely found himself charged with "treasonable practices" but he was not apprehended and there is record of his having addressed what contemporary sources called "a riotous mob" in mid-April of 1782, where he allegedly shouted, "Come on my brave boys, we'll go to the woodpile and get clubs enough to knock their grey whigs off and send them out of the world in an instant." He also said—according to these same sources—that he would "rather fight against this Authority than against the King of Great Britain," but whether Ely really said that or not one cannot be sure. Indeed, the statements of the Elys of the past generally come down through history as rendered by the Dwights.

It is records of the Courts run by the Dwights that normally supply sound evidence as to the fate of the Elys; at any rate in the spring of 1782, Ely was arrested, found guilty of disturbing the peace, fined fifty pounds, and sentenced to six months in prison, and put on a kind of probation—with a bond of two hundred pounds—to keep the peace for three years.

In mid-June, 1782, however, some 150 men, armed but otherwise called "well-behaved," broke into the prison and Ely fled the State. This same Ely is heard of again in September, 1782, where authorities in Vermont arrested him as a "pernicious and seditious man" and he was banished. Massachusetts authorities awaited him and arrested him but he was released on bail.

If Ely remained through the 1780s in Massachusetts, he played no part in the popular unrest that goes by the name of Shays' Rebellion—of which more shortly. Early in the next decade there is record of Ely in Massachusetts' northern district, Maine, where he helped organize so-called squatters who insisted on using the timber belonging to mostly absentee landlords. Some of the buildings owned by these landlords went up in flames rather mysteriously and a writ was issued for the apprehension of Ely but this seems never to have been served; just what became of Samuel Ely thereafter remains a mystery.

Ely's efforts in Massachusetts were but a dress rehearsal for Shays' Rebellion, which rocked the State from 1786 through 1787 and evoked sympathetic responses from thousands in New Hampshire, Vermont, Connecticut and New York. The unrest flowed from economic depression, excessive taxes, merciless creditors and their partisan courts. Indicative are these figures from Worcester County: in 1784 its jail contained eleven persons, of whom seven were there for indebtedness; in 1785 the total number of prisoners in that county's jail came to 103, and of these eighty-six were there for debts, six for nonpayment of taxes, and eleven for all other offenses; in 1786, the jail there held eighty-eight persons, of whom eighty were held for debts, four for nonpayment of taxes and four for all other offenses.

The leaders almost to a man had fought in the Revolution— most of them as privates or noncommissioned officers; this was true of Daniel Shays himself and of Moses Sash, a Black man who held the rank of Captain in the rebellion; it was true of Luke Day and Job Shattuck, Henry Gale and Eli Parsons, of Jason Parmenter and William Whiting—the latter himself a judge in Berkshire county—and of Josiah Whitney, who had risen to the rank of General.

Courts were prevented from sitting, from foreclosing mortgages, and from sentencing honest men to jail for debts that were mountainous and unpaid taxes that were ruinous. Prisons were forcibly opened and such honest men freed. When finally the arsenal at Springfield was besieged, the government brought into play cannon and killed four of the Shaysites and sent the others fleeing. In other engagements during the months that followed the government forces saw three of their men killed and the rebels lost four more; others were wounded. Guerrilla warfare appeared throughout western Massachusetts and homes and barns went up in flames. Government forces tried to intimidate the womenfolk of the rebels and failed; in at least one case the rescue of such a rebel from a jail was done by a force of men and one woman. Supplies needed by often desperate rebels, holding out in a New England winter, came from the women. After the fighting, when a dozen were scheduled to die by hanging, it was the women who led in organizing a campaign for clemency and traveled many a weary mile to plead for mercy from the rulers in Boston.

Popular support was present, not only in Massachusetts but in all the New England states and in New York. The Governor, James Bowdoin, who had been ready with warrants for arrest and execution and proclamations of rewards for the bodies of named rebels, was defeated in the elections of 1787 and replaced by John Hancock, whose sympathies were more democratic. The vote was a resounding 18,500 for Hancock and 6,400 for Bowdoin—and this despite the fact that Bowdoin's rulings had led to the disfranchisement of many of those who had followed Shays.

Under Hancock, all those condemned to hang were spared, except one man—and in that case the man's guilt of theft perhaps counted more than that of rebellion. All others, including Shays himself, finally were fully pardoned; Shays lived on, as a farmer in upstate New York, until his eighty-fourth year, dying in 1825. The legislature of Massachusetts in the fall of 1787 removed the civil disabilities which had been placed upon rebel participants and, more important, passed "An Act for the Relief of Poor Prisoners who were committed by Execution for Debt," which provided freedom for one so jailed if he could take an oath to his poverty and inability to pay.

This rebellion was clearly one of class versus class—of poor versus rich and specifically of the debtors against the creditors. It was one, therefore, which witnessed major use of military force with that force especially mustered and paid for with funds earmarked for the purpose by the rich in the East. Its nature was deeper than that of the rebellion against Britain as it represented at its core a threat to the sanctity of private property and of contracts based upon such ownership. Even Samuel Adams, therefore, who was a chief engineer of the rebellion against Britain and who was to be a partisan of the French Revolution, was a strong opponent of the Shays' effort; it was aimed not only against the authority of a republican form of government—which Adams had done so much to establish—but it also was one that threatened "civilization" itself, insofar as it attacked basic legal bulwarks of the private ownership of the means of production.

General Henry Knox wrote to Washington in 1786 that the rebellious farmers held views that were most dangerous and pernicious. "Their creed is," he declared,

> That the property of the United States has been protected from the confiscations of Britain by the joint exertions of all, and therefore ought to be the common property of all. And he that attempts opposition to this creed is an enemy to equity and justice, and ought to be swept from off the face of the earth.

Briefly, Knox went on with manifest horror:

> In a word, they are determined to annihilate all debts, public and
> private, and have agrarian laws, which are easily effected by means
> of unfunded paper money which shall be a tender in all cases
> whatever.

Of the outstanding Revolutionary leaders, only Thomas Jefferson reacted to the Shays' outbreak with calm and a touch of
real sympathy. It was in response to that event that he
suggested—from his ministerial post in France—that the outbreak surely was "not entirely without excuse" and, later, that its
occurrence would seem to indicate that those who governed had
become "inattentive to public affairs" and that when this happened, even "Congress and assemblies, judges and convention,
shall all become wolves." He added, in this letter of January 16,
1787, that having been in Europe and seen how their governments function he could only think in terms of wolves, "for I can
apply no milder term . . . to the general prey of the rich on the
poor." Writing on January 30, 1787, again from Paris, this time
to James Madison, he remarked that "turbulence" might well
mark a form of government where popular will was influential,
but this turbulence was useful, because:

> It prevents the degeneracy of government, and nourishes a
> general attention to the public affairs. I hold it, that a little
> rebellion, now and then, is a good thing, and as necessary in the
> political world as storms in the physical. Unsuccessful rebellions,
> indeed, generally establish the encroachments on the rights of the
> people, which have produced them. An observation of this truth
> should render honest republican governors so mild in their pun-
> ishment of rebellions, as not to discourage them too much. It is a
> medicine necessary for the sound health of government.

That was the best of the statements from one of the best
among the leaders of eighteenth-century United States, among
the leaders of the young Republic. But how severe were the
limitations of even this best of the rulers, was shown by this same
leader, thirteen years later, when he wrote to his sorely troubled
friend, James Monroe, the Governor of Virginia.

Monroe was chief executive officer of Virginia when the State was unnerved by the uncovering and crushing of the great slave conspiracy involving many hundreds, led by the twenty-one-year old blacksmith, Gabriel, slave of one, Prosser. Monroe, veteran of the Revolution and disciple of Jefferson, had personally interviewed the rebel leaders and found them staunch revolutionists; none would inform on their fellows. "How shall I act," he asked Jefferson, in a letter dated September 15, 1800, "now that many have been convicted and sentenced to hang—to hang for demanding freedom?" Jefferson, soon to take office as President, replied five days later urging on Monroe what mercy he could exercise, consistent with his office, for the world at large "cannot lose sight of the rights of the two parties, and the object of the unsuccessful one."

In the case of Shays, one man died on the gallows; in the case of Gabriel—where the source of the "little rebellion" was actual enslavement—thirty-five were executed. Still, Monroe, prodded by Jefferson and one hopes by his conscience, did reprieve some others who also had been sentenced to death. In this case, however, such reprieve meant sale into slavery in the West Indies and whether or not those spared death were grateful for this "mercy" is a matter on which they were never able to express an opinion.

Conclusion

WITH the mid-1790s, the young Republic was at the threshold of a new epoch. The Revolution, the Confederation, the making of the Constitution were history; the viability of the Republic seemed sure. Before the nation lay the challenge of a revolutionary and Napoleonic Europe which would decisively affect its internal and international affairs. The westward movement would intensify and with it fierce Indian resistance; technical improvements in 1793 and 1795 opened up vast possibilities for cotton and sugar production, with fateful impact upon the slave-plantation system, the Afro-American people in particular and the country's future as a whole.

From the ascendancy of Washington-Hamilton to that of Jefferson-Madison was less than a decade, but it was a transition of major dimensions. A fourth volume will tell that fateful story.

Reference Notes

Chapter I

[1]Josiah Tucker, *Cui Bono?* . . . 3rd edition, London, 1782, pp. 117–18.
[2]Herbert Aptheker, *The Colonial Era*, New York, International Publishers, new edition, 1966.
[3]This was always part of the "New World" concept. Thus, Francis Bacon's *Novum Organum* (1620): "Even if the breath of hope which blows on us from that New Continent were fainter than it is and harder to perceive, yet the trial (if we would not bear a spirit altogether abject) must by all means be made . . . there is hope enough and to spare, not only to make a bold man try, but also to make a sober-minded and wise man to believe."
[4]The idea of the masses of people—that is, poor, working people—as literally other than human, recurs in literature from Chaucer in the fourteenth century to Edmund Spenser in the sixteenth to Voltaire and Alexander Hamilton in the eighteenth. In intensified form it reappears in racist writing and is present also in male-supremacist theorizing. The present writer published a brief analysis of this matter in *Political Affairs*, April, 1975.

Chapter II

[1]This picture of an absence of poverty and the presence of rather universal well-being (among white people) is quite mythological, as later evidence will show; but the existence—and persistence—of the myth is undeniable.
[2]Characteristic of the view of the Left on this matter was that expressed by the English radical, Richard Price, in a letter to Benjamin Rush, January 26, 1787: "It is a pity that some general controllable power cannot be established of sufficient vigour to decide disputes, to regulate commerce, to prevent wars, and to constitute a union that shall have weight and credit. At present, the power of Congress is, in Europe, an object of derision rather than respect."

Chapter III

[1]"The disposition to give to the new system all the vigour consistent with Republican principles, was not a little stimulated by a backwardness in some quarters towards a Convention for the purpose, which was ascribed to a secret dislike to popular Government and a hope that delay would bring it more into disgrace and pave the way for a form of Government more congenial with monarchical or aristocratical predilections."—James Madison to J. G. Jackson, December 27, 1821.

151

Chapter IV

¹This procedure is spelled out in some detail, for one often finds statements like the following: "The men at Philadelphia . . . decided not to transmit the fruit of their labors to the Congress under whose authority they had convened, but directly to the people."—Leo Pfeffer, *The Liberties of an American* (Beacon Press, Boston, 1956) p. 3.

²Beard himself partially acknowledged this, in the book's preface, by pointing to the work of S. B. Harding, C. H. Ambler, O. G. Libby, A. M. Simons, and Gustavus Myers.

³*The United States: A Democracy in World Perspective* (1947), pp. 68–69. J. Allen Smith, in the already cited work, published forty years earlier, had written: "The long list of distinguished men who took part in the deliberation of that body is noteworthy, however, for the absence of such names as Samuel Adams, Thomas Jefferson, Thomas Paine, Patrick Henry and other democratic leaders of that time."—p. 33.

⁴Robert E. Thomas makes this suggestion in his valuable essay, "Reappraisal of Beard's *Economic Interpretation of the Constitution*," in the *American Historical Review*, January 1952. This author correctly reminds readers of Beard's pro-Federalist and conservative views at the time he wrote his book; but he misses the main reason for the book's disturbing impact when he ascribes it to "misinterpretation."

⁵This is not the occasion for a detailed analysis of the historical writings of Charles Beard. Very briefly, however, Beard pictured the origins of the Constitution in Madisonian, not Marxian, terms. He adopted the idea of the state as a balance wheel, an umpire, in the midst of contending classes, especially contending *propertied* classes. In this sense, Beard's critique never got beyond the muckraking level, and so had strong appeal to reformist groups.

⁶Merrill Jensen, *The Articles of Confederation* (1940), p. 245, characterized the Constitution as "a conservative counter-revolution." In his more recent *The New Nation* (1950) he moderated his language, but does not significantly amend his estimate.

Chapter V

¹Only James Wilson, of Pennsylvania, disagreed. In the Convention, on July 13, 1787, he said, according to Madison's notes: "He could not agree that property was the sole or the primary object of Government and Society. The cultivation and improvement of the human mind was the most noble object."

²The class bias with which this was and is enforced need not detain us at this point. Suffice it here to point out that combinations known as corporations were legal, but combinations known as trade unions were conspiratorial and illegal. Marx pointed out: "By the decree of June 14, 1791, it (the French bourgeoisie) declared that any combination among the workers was 'an attack upon liberty and upon the Declaration of the Rights of Man' "—punishable by fine and loss of citizenship rights for one year. *Capital* (International Publishers, 1967, Vol. I, pp. 821–22n.)

Chapter VI

[1]Including women and all peoples of color—probably not in Beard's mind.

[2]Franklin, in his characteristically far-sighted way, also reminded his fellow delegates of world opinion. Said he: "This Constitution will be much read and attended to in Europe, and if it should betray a great partiality to the rich will not only hurt us in the esteem of the most liberal and enlightened men there, but discourage the common people from removing into this country."

[3]Something of the consequence of this for contemporaries is conveyed by the fact that in 1787 in New York City, a play called *The Contrast*, written by a Revolutionary Army veteran, Royall Tyler, was being presented; in its prologue were these lines:

> *Exult each patriot heart! this night is shewn*
> *A piece, which we may fairly call our own;*
> *Where the proud titles of 'My Lord!' 'Your Grace!'*
> *To humble Mr. and plain Sir give place.*

[4]Some of the details of this history and problems of its application are discussed in the work of Zechariah Chafee. He, and other authors on this subject, fail to mention the widespread practice in southern states, before the Civil War, of outlawing bands of fugitive slaves.

[5]For an analysis of the much less liberal views of treason then current in Great Britain, see Bradley Chapin, "The American Revolution as Lese Majesty," in *The Pennsylvania Magazine of History* (July, 1955) LXXIX, pp. 310–330.

[6]Thus, during World War II, the writ did several hundred thousand American citizens of Japanese origin no good at all; nor did it help those jailed at the same time in England because Parliament had authorized jailing on the mere say-so of a Cabinet Minister. Again, while the McCarran Act specifically affirmed the writ, it simultaneously authorized the arrest and indefinite detention of "Communists" and others who may be suspected by the Attorney General of being *potential* saboteurs!

[7]Especially helpful on this point and on the misuse of the veto power by later Presidents, particularly Gerald Ford, is Edward Pessen's "The Arrogant Veto," in *The Nation*, August 30, 1975.

[8]Note that Jefferson, in his *Notes on Virginia*, warned of the dangers in an "elective despotism," and praised "those benefits" produced by a "proper complication of principles."

[9]This idea is frequently expressed, quite often by those who desire a curtailment of democratic rights. An example is Alan Valentine, *The Age of Conformity* (Regnery, Chicago, 1954). A good historical refutation of this position is in H. S. Commager, *Majority Rule and Minority Rights* (Oxford Univ. Press, N.Y., 1953).

[10]We will examine, in subsequent pages, the limitations of this, but the fundamentally *popular* nature of the republican form is central.

[11]This originally appeared in volume 27 of the *Political Science Quarterly*. It is reprinted in part 1 of Robert G. McCloskey, ed., *Essays in Constitutional History* (Knopf, N.Y., 1957).

[12]See: Irving Brant, *James Madison: Father of the Constitution* (Bobbs-Merrill, Indianapolis, 1950) pp. 16–17,234. This is of some relevance to those historians who have expressed doubts as to whether "breeding" existed during slavery.

[13]Herbert Aptheker, *The American Revolution, 1763–1783*, New York, International Publishers, 1960.

[14]The omission was of considerable practical significance. Thus, Frederick Douglass cited it, and the reason for it, plus the general humanistic content of the Constitution, in his battle against Garrison's very sectarian "damn the Constitution," anarchistic attitude. It may have given Garrison some satisfaction to burn the Constitution in public, but that was a strange way to build a mass movement. Douglass was correct, both as to his evaluation of the Constitution, and his tactical approach.

Chapter VIII

[1]In the early federal period, the Treasury Department had a much more numerous staff than any other Cabinet post; thus, in Washington's first administration, Hamilton had an assistant, a controller, a treasurer, an auditor, a register and thirty-five clerks as well as about one thousand customhouse officers and internal revenue agents; State, on the other hand, had four clerks, a messenger and an office keeper, while the War Department had three clerks.

Chapter IX

[1]The Ordinance reflected the intent of dominant forces in the East to protect their own supremacy in the new section. That is, by limiting the number of new States that might be created to five and by providing no self-rule during the early territorial stage and giving the governor an absolute veto power during the second stage of territorial status, the frontiersmen felt they were without effective political power. In tune also with the politically conservative intent of the Congress that framed the 1787 Ordinance, was the provision that adult males would require the ownership of at least fifty acres of land in order to vote and that members of the territorial legislatures had to possess a minimum of two hundred acres.

[2]This referred to treaties made in 1784 and 1785 with separate Indian peoples wherein land was supposed to be conveyed to the United States without any compensation to those doing the conveying. Extreme dissatisfaction resulted and rumors of impending Indian wars reached the ears of Congress; this was part of the origin of the 1787 Ordinance.

[3]Partially to placate the West, Washington chose Jefferson, rather than Jay, as his Secretary of State. John Jay had been the Secretary for Foreign Affairs under the Confederacy; the appointment of Jefferson was understood as a rebuke to Jay for his agreeing to surrender New Orleans in the Jay-Gardoqui proposal.

Chapter X

[1]A Black woman, later known as Elizabeth Freeman, born a slave in Massachusetts, was severely beaten and fled in 1780. Her owner sought her return, but she refused and obtained the assistance of a well-known attorney, Theodore Sedgwick. Through Sedgwick, Elizabeth Freeman brought suit against the owner—one Colonel John Ashley—asserting that the Bill of Rights of the State's Constitution outlawed slavery. The case was heard in Great Barrington and the jury ruled, in 1781, in her favor; it not only affirmed Elizabeth Freeman's

freedom but ordered the Colonel to pay her thirty shillings as damages. Elizabeth Freeman thus was responsible for the judicial ending of slavery in Massachusetts; she died in Great Barrington in 1829 when about eighty-five years of age. (On this, see Sidney Kaplan, *The Black Presence in the Era of the American Revolution*, Greenwich, Conn., New York Graphic Society, Ltd., 1973, pp. 216–17).

[2]"Constantia" was Judith Sargent Murray of Gloucester, Mass. Her father was a wealthy merchant and supporter of the Revolution and the movement for the Constitution. Her portrait was painted by both Copley and Stuart and she moved in top circles of her day, being at times the guest of President and Mrs. Washington. See Vena B. Field, *Constantia* (Orono, Maine, Univ. of Maine Studies (1933), 2nd series, #17); Eleanor Flexner, *Century of Struggle* (1959), pp. 15–17. "Constantia's" 1790 essay is reprinted in Aileen S. Kraditor, *Up From the Pedestal* (1968), pp. 30–37.

Chapter XI

[1]Note the remarks of Raymond A. Mohl: "The idea of early America as a land of opportunity deserves serious reconsideration . . . Surely the society of preindustrial America, and especially the urban ingredient of that society, requires closer scrutiny before the cliche of America as the land of opportunity can be accepted at face value." *Poverty in New York, 1783–1825* (New York, Oxford University Press, 1971).

Bibliography

COLLECTIONS OF SOURCES:

WRITINGS, LETTERS, DOCUMENTS

Letters, papers and writings of leading figures during the decade include—
with the names of the editors:

Adams, Abigail (Charles Francis Adams); *Adams, John* (Charles Francis Adams);
Franklin, Benjamin (Albert H. Smyth); *Hamilton, Alexander* (Harold C. Syrett
and Jacob E. Cooke); *Jefferson, Thomas* (Julian P. Boyd); *Madison, James*
(Gaillard Hunt); *Monroe, James* (S. M. Hamilton); *Paine, Thomas* (Philip S.
Foner); *Rush, Benjamin* (Lyman H. Butterfield); *Washington, George* (John C.
Fitzpatrick).

Collections of important public documents include:

Antifederalist Papers, edited by Morton Borden (1965)
Anti-Federalists Versus Federalists, edited by John D. Lewis (1967)
Debates in the Several State Conventions on the Adoption of the Federal Constitution,
  edited by Jonathan Elliot (1861–63)
Documents Illustrative of the Formation of the Union of the American States, edited by
  Charles C. Tansill (1927)
Federalist, The, edited by Benjamin F. Wright (1961)
Records of the Federal Convention of 1787, edited by Max Farrand (1911)
*Treaties between the United States of America and the Several Indian Tribes, from 1778
  to 1837* (1838)

COLLECTIONS OF HISTORICAL DOCUMENTS IN SPECIFIC AREAS:

Aptheker, Herbert, ed., *A Documentary History of the Negro People in the United
  States*, Vol. I (1951)
Commager, Henry S., ed., *Documents of American History* (4th edit., 1948)
Hofstadter, Richard, ed., *Great Issues in American History, 1765–1865* (1958)
Kraditor, Aileen, ed., *Up From the Pedestal* (1968)
Schappes, Morris U., ed., *Documentary History of the Jews in the United States* (1950)

GENERAL HISTORIES

Beard, Charles A. and Mary R. Beard, *Basic History of the United States* (1944)
Burns, Edward M., *The American Idea of Mission* (1957)
Chambers, William N., *Political Parties in a New Nation: The American Experience*
  (1963)

Channing, Edward, *A History of the United States*, Vol. IV (1917)

Curti, Merle, *The Growth of American Thought* (3rd edit., 1964)

Dorfman, Joseph, *The Economic Mind in American Civilization, 1606–1865* (2 vols., 1946)

Ferguson, E. James, *The Power of the Purse: A History of American Public Finance, 1776–1790* (1961)

Greene, Evarts B., *The Revolutionary Generation, 1763–1790* (1943)

Hacker, Louis M., *The Triumph of American Capitalism* (1940)

Hildreth, Richard, *The History of the United States of America* (6 vols., The Bradley edit., n.d.,) Vols. III, IV

Jensen, Merrill, *The New Nation* (1950)

McMaster, John B., *History of the People of the United States from the Revolution to the Civil War* (8 vols., 1911 edit), Vols. I,II

Miller, John C., *The Federalist Era* (1960)

Nettels, Curtis P., *The Emergence of a National Economy* (1962)

Nye, Russel B., *Cultural Life of the New Nation: 1767–1830* (1960)

Robinson, Donald L., *Slavery in the Structure of American Politics, 1765–1820* (1971)

Schachner, Nathan, *The Founding Fathers* (1954)

Wright, Esmond, *Fabric of Freedom, 1763–1800* (1961)

BIOGRAPHIES

Baker, Leonard, *John Marshall: A Life in Law* (1974)

Brant, Irving, *James Madison: Father of the Constitution* (1950)

Burns, E. M., *James Madison: Philosopher of the Constitution* (1938)

Cone, Carl B., *Torchbearer of Freedom: The Influence of Richard Price on Eighteenth Century Thought* (1952)

Drake, Francis S., *Life and Correspondence of Henry Knox* (1873)

Field, Vena B., *Constantia* (1933)

Flexner, James T., *George Washington and the New Nation (1783–1793)* (1970)

Foster, William O., *James Jackson, 1757–1806* (1960)

Koch, Adrienne, *Jefferson and Madison* (1950)

Malone, Dumas, *Jefferson and the Rights of Man* (1951)

Miller, John C., *Sam Adams: Pioneer in Propaganda* (1936)

Mitchell, Broadus, *Alexander Hamilton: The National Adventure, 1788–1804* (1962)

Schachner, Nathan, *Thomas Jefferson* (1951)

Smith, Charles Page, *James Wilson, Founding Father: 1742–1798* (1956)

Smith, Page, *John Adams* (2 vols., 1962)

Van Doren, Carl, *Benjamin Franklin* (1938)

Wilder, E. W., *George Clinton* (1938)

SPECIAL STUDIES

Adair, Douglass, "Politics Reduced to Science: Hume, Madison and the Tenth *Federalist*," Huntington Library Quarterly (1957), 20:343–60

Aptheker, Herbert, *American Negro Slave Revolts* (1943)

Bancroft, George, *History of the Formation of the Constitution* (1885)

Beard, Charles A., *An Economic Interpretation of the Constitution of the United States* (1913; 1962 edit.)

Berkhofer, Robert F., "Barrier to Settlement: British Indian Policy in the Old Northwest, 1783–1794," in D. M. Ellis, ed., *The Frontier in American Development* (1969)

Bishop, H. M., "Why Rhode Island Opposed the Federal Constitution," *Rhode Island History* (1949), 8:1–14

Brown, E. Francis, "Documents: Shays Rebellion," *American Historical Review* (1931), 36:776–78

Brown, Robert E., *Charles Beard and the Constitution: A Critical Analysis of an Economic Interpretation of the Constitution* (1956)

Calhoun, Arthur W., *The Worker Looks at Government* (1927)

Chafee, Zechariah, *How Human Rights Got Into the Constitution* (1952)
Three Human Rights in the Constitution (1956)

Chapin, Bradley, "The American Revolution as Lese Majesty," *Pennsylvania Magazine of History* (1955), 69:310–30

Commager, Henry S., *Majority Rule and Minority Rights* (1943)

Crowl, Philip A., "Anti-Federalism in Maryland," *William & Mary Quarterly* (1947), 4:446–60

Dietz, G., *The Federalist: A Classic on Federalism & Free Government* (1960)

Du Bois, W. E. B., *The Suppression of the African Slave Trade* (1896; Kraus edition, edited by H. Aptheker, 1975)

Dumond, Dwight L., *Anti-Slavery: The Crusade for Freedom in America* (1961)

Dunbar, Louise B., *A Study of 'Monarchical' Tendencies in the United States: 1776 to 1801* (1922)

Dyer, Walter A., "Embattled Farmers," *New England Quarterly* (1931), 4:460–81 (on the Shays Rebellion)

East, Robert A., "The Massachusetts Conservatives in the Critical Period," in R. B. Morris, ed., *The Era of the American Revolution* (1939)

Eblen, Jack E., *The First and Second United States Empires: Governors and Territorial Governments, 1784–1912* (1968)

Feer, Robert A., "Imprisonment for Debt in Massachusetts before 1800," *Mississippi Valley Historical Review* (1961), 48:252–69
"Shays's Rebellion and the Constitution: A Study in Causation," *New England Quarterly* (1969), 42:388–410

Ferguson, E. James, "The Nationalists of 1781–1783 and the Economic Interpretation of the Constitution," *Journal of American History* (1969), 56:241–56

Fiske, John, *The Critical Period of American History* (1888)

Flexner, Eleanor, *Century of Struggle: The Woman's Rights Movement in the United States* (1959)

Foner, Philip S., *History of the Labor Movement in the United States*, Vol. I (1947)

Franklin, John Hope, *From Slavery to Freedom: A History of Negro Americans* (1947; 4th edit., 1974)

Fraser, Leon, *English Opinion of the American Constitution and Government* (1915)

Hindle, Brooke, *The Pursuit of Science in Revolutionary America, 1735–1789* (1956)

Hofstadter, Richard, "Charles Beard and the Constitution," in Howard K. Beale, ed., *Charles A. Beard: An Appraisal* (1954)

Holcombe, Arthur N., *Our More Perfect Union: From Eighteenth-Century Principles to Twentieth Century Practise* (1950)
"Sections, Classes and the Federal Constitution," in *Gaspar G. Bacon Lectures on the Constitution* (1953)

Horsman, Reginald, *Expansion and American Indian Policy, 1783-1812* (1967)

Josephy, Alvin M., Jr., *The Indian Heritage of America* (1963)

Kaplan, Sidney, "A Negro Veteran in Shays' Rebellion," *The Journal of Negro History* (1948), 33:123-29

    " 'Honestus' and the Annihilation of Lawyers," *South Atlantic Quarterly* (1949), 48:401-420

    The Black Presence in the Era of the American Revolution, 1770-1800 (1973)

    "The Ely Outbreaks in Northampton: Prelude to Shays Rebellion," in H. U.

Faulkner, ed., *The Northampton Book: Chapters from Three Hundred Years in the Life of a New England Town* (1954)

Kelly, Alfred H. and W. A. Harbison, *The American Constitution*, Vol. I (1948)

Kenyon, Cecelia M., "Men of Little Faith," *William & Mary Quarterly* (1955), 3:112-32

Kulikoff, Allan, "The Progress of Inequality in Revolutionary Boston," *William & Mary Quarterly* (1971), 28:375-412

Lynd, Staughton, "The Mechanics in New York City Politics, 1774-1788," *Labor History* (1964), 5:225-46

Lynd, Staughton and Alfred Young, "The Mechanics and New York City Politics, 1774-1801," *Labor History* (1964), 5:215-24

Lynd, S., *Class Conflict, Slavery and the United States Constitution: Ten Essays* (1967)

Main, Jackson T., *The Anti-Federalists: Critics of the Constitution* (1961)

    Social Structure of Revolutionary America (1965)

    "Trends in Wealth Concentration before 1860," *Journal of Economic History* (1971), 31:445-47

McCloskey, Robert G., ed., *Essays in Constitutional History* (1957)

McCormick, Richard P., *Experiment in Independence: New Jersey in the Critical Period, 1781-1789* (1950)

McDonald, Forrest, *We, the People: The Economic Origins of the Constitution* (1958)

McIlwaine, Charles H., *Constitutionalism: Ancient and Modern* (1940)

McNickle, D'Arcy, *They Came Here First: The Epic of the American Indian* (1949)

Mohl, Raymond A., *Poverty in New York, 1783-1825* (1971)

Moody, Robert E., "Samuel Ely; Forerunner of Shays," *New England Quarterly* (1932), 5:105-134

Morris, Richard B., "The Confederation Period and the American Historian," *William & Mary Quarterly* (1956), 3:139-51

Pessen, Edward, *Riches, Class, and Power Before the Civil War* (1973)

Peterson, Merrill D., "Jefferson and Commercial Policy, 1783-1793," *William & Mary Quarterly* (1965), 22:584-610

Risford, N. K. and G. DenBoer, "The Evolution of Political Parties in Virginia, 1782-1800," *Journal of American History* (1974), 60:961-84

Roll, C. W., Jr., "We, Some of the People: Apportionment in Thirteen State Conventions Ratifying the Convention," *Journal of American History* (1969), 56:21-40

Rutland, Robert A., *The Birth of the Bill of Rights, 1776-1791* (1955)

Schuyler, Robert L., *The Constitution of the United States: An Historical Survey* (1923)

Smith, J. Allen, *The Spirit of American Government* (1907)

Smith, Jonathan, "The Depression of 1785 and Shays' Rebellion," *William & Mary Quarterly* (1948), 5:77-94

Soltow, Lee, ed., *Six Papers on the Size, Distribution of Wealth and Income* (1961) "Economic Inequality in the United States, 1790–1860," *Journal of Economic History* (1971), 31:822–39

Starkey, Marion L., *A Little Rebellion* (1955); (on Shays' Rebellion)

Struik, Dirk J., *Yankee Science in the Making* (1948)

Underhill, Ruth M., *Red Man's America: A History of Indians in the United States* (1953)

Vaughan, Alden T., "The 'Horrid and Unnatural Rebellion' of Daniel Shays," *American Heritage* (1966), 4:51–53, 77–81

Warren, Charles, *The Supreme Court in United States History* (2 vols., rev. edit., 1937)

Warren, Joseph, "Documents Relating to the Shays Rebellion," *American Historical Review* (1898), 2:693–99

Washburn, Wilcomb E., *The Indian in America* (1975)

Wright, Benjamin F., *The Growth of American Constitutional Law* (1942)

Young, Alfred, "The Mechanics and the Jeffersonians, 1789–1801," *Labor History* (1964), 5:247–76

Zornow, William F., "New York Tariff Policies, 1775–1789," *New York History* (1956), 37:40–63

Index